the
Mayas

the
Mayas

life, culture and art
through the experiences
of a man of the time

Demetrio Sodi M.

with colaboration of
Adela Fernández

PANORAMA EDITORIAL, S.A.

Sixth edition in english: 1987
© Panorama Editorial, S.A.
Leibnitz 31, Col. Anzures
11590 México, D.F.

PANORAMA SERIES
Under the direction of:
Federico Santiago E.

Translated by:
Elizabeth M. Plaister

Drawings by:
José Narro

Printed in Mexico
Impreso en México

ISBN 968-38-0041-6 English
ISBN 968-38-0040-8 Spanish

Index

Introductión

One of the paradoxical attitudes of XX century man is to hark back to the past with wonder and profound nostalgia; paradoxical because all his efforts are meanwhile concentrated on the future, not only for the purpose of relating to it but also of recreating himself within it. Contemporary man, who is highly Westernized and a firm believer in the progress of science, seeks to win eternity. These are the roots of the duality of his quest: simultaneously in communion with the future and deeply rooted in the past.

This return to the past does not originate solely in a thirst for culture and the pleasure of accumulating knowledge passed down through time but may also be accounted for by man's desire to make of time an enclave to ensure his place in the absolute: "I am everything that ever has been and ever will be".

This aspiration to permanence and immensity, longing for both the past and the future, produces an inebration of All. Such an inebration engendered by totality, or infinite wholeness cannot exist in the absence of intellectual and emotional contact with previous worlds. This accounts for the fascination of history and of archeological remains which carry us back to cultures that have been lost or changed with the passing of the centuries.

To penetrate the Mayan universe is to journey into the awe-inspiring sublimeness of a people obsessed by time. Hence, it is not difficult to understand how it is that the Mayan region enslaves those who study or visit it since its mysteries are none other than those inherent in time itself. Stone, hewn by man to create steles and temples, is a living voice which fully recounts the evolution of their way of thinking: the Mayan conception of the universe, ever linked to the values of all that is ephimeral and eternal.

The Mayan period was one of the richest in intellectual achievement. Science and art were used as formulae to explain human existence, life and death. We find in the Mayan culture, as in many other ancient cultures, that man is an animated being in a type of planesphere; a being originating from the earth and aspiring to the heavens and required in life to solve the dilemma of his existence in the dialectic established between human and divine.

This book attempts to delve into the behind-the-scenes history uncovered by various scientists in their research but seeking to emphasize the passage of Mayan life on the bais of its standars, customs and beliefs: everyday as an expression of their deepest philosophical thought.

For this purpose, the genre of the novel or even of the short story, provides a wide range of possibilities for amply recounting the human aspect of any culture. In such a case, the word acquires a greater responsibility in the sense that on the basis of scientific and with artistic license, it develops an aesthetic happening.

The tale recounts the life of a family, clearly situated in time and space (the post-classical period in the Yucatan peninsula). This makes it difficult to chronologically follow the entire historical role of the Mayas. Nonetheless, in view of the magical thought of this culture and its enormous sense of the registering of events, it has been possible to tackle the question of time through references to the past, present and future.

Our characters are linked to the past through steles, murals and historical teachings, through the exercise of mnemotechny which was taught by the elder members of the community to the youths with the aim of preserving ancient texts. The whole is reinforced with evocations originating from the permanent cult to their ancestors.

The reading of the future through the observation of cosmic cycles and events which repeat themselves (an example being the tables of the eclipses) and the magic premonitionary visions of the augurs, the reading of the waters in the sacred cenotes and of the oracles together allowed events to be anticipated, ranging from the break down of the Confederation of Mayapán and the subsequent hegemony, to the arrival of the Spaniards.

The birth

Ix Cuzam Chi was about to give birth to her first son when her husband Ah Tzab Kumun, noble servant of the priests, left to seek the necessary helpers. All knew that the event was imminent and therefore the midwife and her assistants were soon ready and were not long in arriving.

No sooner had the women entered the house than they spread a white cloth on the floor, arranged the medicinal herbs, lit the braziers and burned *pom,* aromatic resins.

While the mother summoned up all her courage and strength to bring her fruit of flesh and dreams into the world, Ah Tzab Kumun had gone outside and stood gazing at the heavenly vault. Shaken by the miracle of life, he reflected fearfully on the type of fate the divinities had in store for his son.

Inside, the women concentrated all their efforts into

bringing the new being into the world. In the four corners of the room, the midwife had placed images of Ixchel, godess and protector of childbirth. She rubbed the body of the mother, all the while intoning propitiatory prayers and incantations. She invoked the sun, the sea, the jaguar and the serpent, that they might give strength to the unborn child. She bore down on the mother's stomach in order to transmit to the child all that life in the world meant and to protect it from the shock of birth. She spoke to the child of wind, light and space where it would have to make its own way. She spoke of pain and joy, work, care, tolerance and especially of the child's duty to the gods.

She told the child that it is difficult to be a man because man is not born to spread confusion but to throw light on mysteries; not to compete with the gods but to honour them; not only to enjoy beauty and the gifts of nature but also to create his own beauty; to build a human world in nature. The experience of birth is painful but life itself is its recompense.

"Come into the world", the midwife told the child, "Your hour of light and air has come! The time has come for you to be astonished because you will see soon enough that life is indeed astonishing! Have no fear, the gods give comfort and the great men will guide you. Come into the world! It is your time to come to earth!"

As though drawn by the fascination of these words, the child's head appeared and, with the mother's final strength, the tiny body was projected into the world. Its cry filled Cuzam with emotion and, sweating and exhausted, she turned to look upon her child. The women continued their task of cleaning the mother and child and began to sing of one accord. They took the ashes from the hearth and there dug a hole in which they buried the placenta so that the infant would be protected by the Ancient God of Fire.

A short while later they told Ah Tzab Kumun that he had fathered a son. Moved, he took up his conch and blew upon it with unprecendented strength. The prolonged sound travelled through the air, proclaiming to the gods the good fortune and gratitude of human beings who reproduce and with their own blood create new beings.

Hu, the moon, shone in the lofty hights of the three skies. It is the same godess Ixchel who, moments before, protected the birth. Light also shone out from other godesses of the firmament such as *Xaman Ek,* the deity protecting travellers and merchants (the polar star) and *Noh Ek,* the planet Venus. Soon they would hide themselves when *Kin,* the sun, after overcoming the shadows and dark deities in combat, would arise from the Underworld.

"*Moved, he took up his conch and blew a note with unprecendented strength...*"

Predestination

When a child was born, tradition required a ceremony to be held, presided by a high-ranking member of the priesthood, to clarify the desingss of the gods for the new-born infant. Man came to earth to fulfill a specific destiny, to remain there a limited time and to carry out a precise function. Man was his own instrument but this instrument was directed by the will of the gods. They guided it and dictated its destiny and its form, its voice and strength and it was man's duty to follow the road he was shown.

Many were the tasks that men came to earth to fulfill but each individual had his own specific role in order to ensure a global harmony. When these specific duties were satisfactorily fulfilled, neither god nor man wanted for anything. The whole universe was provided for.

Ah Tzab and Cuzam brought their offerings to the

priests. The mother cradled the infant in her arms while the aged augur stared deep into the child's eyes as though gazing into two clear pools brimming with images. Then he smiled with such evident satisfaction that it brought joy to the hearts of the parents. The priest gave a signal and a musician began to play the *tunkul*. All present bowed deeply to the four cardinal points in greeting to the gods from each corner of the universe.

Before the silent devotion of those in attendance, the elder intoned his prayers. Then he seated himself before his books and carefully consulted the date of the *Tzolkin*, the ritual calendar, corresponding to the date of the *Haab*, the solar calendar. He raised his eyes from the written pages and murmured the date of the birth: I *Ahaud* 8 *Cumkú*. Next he gave the child his first name: *Keh* (deer). Additions were later made to this totemic name, because a name was something that grows and changes with the passing of time and the change of age and profession.

Every human being had another *I*, an animal spirit which lived within him and gave him his zoological characteristics. Hence, having these two complementary forces within him, man was better equipped to fulfill his destiny. Being a sacred animal, the deer was a good protective spirit for the infant. He would have a valuable intercessor before the gods and many would be the days in each year when his creative powers would excel, especially during the season when this species reproduced (April to June).

The priest passed the incense over the child's body, making signs with the smoke and impregnating him with the scent. He warned the parents of the days on which the child could come to harm and of the unpleasant experiences to which he would be subject. He described to the parents how they could free the child from the forces of evil and how to attract good to him. He foretold which periods would be favourable for the child and instructed the parents in the ways of maintaining and increasing the favour of the gods. He gave them a sheet of amate paper, feathers and coloured earth. This meant that their son would paint the codices which was a highly valued task because upon this depended the recording of history and all knowledge.

To a certain extent, Ah Tzab Kumun was also privileged because, while assisting in the preparations for the great ceremonies, he was in close contact with the high-ranking dignitaries and the gods, but he was forbidden to touch the sacred books. Now, however, his son Keh would have access to all knowledge. He would sit with the wise men, listening to their ideas so as to be able to put them down in the codices. They would teach him to understand things because a skill n painting was not sufficient, an ability to comprehend was also essential. For all these reasons, his parents were overjoyed. The instruments given to them by the priest also had to be buried under the ashes of the hearth in order to guarantee and protect the activity pronounced for their son. The ceremony came to a close with all present again bowing deeply to the four cardinal points.

A sense of beauty

"Beauty is a duty", said the elders, "because our appearance must be pleasant to the eyes that behold us". For this reason, a great deal of effort was put into achieving an agreeable personal image. Cleanliness, care in dressing and certain features of grace and delicacy all served to improve the appearance.

Scarcely four days after Keh was born, his mother, who had laid him naked on a small reed bed, placed one board behind his head and another against his forehead and tied then tighly together in order to flatten his head in accordance with the noble tradition. Since his bones were still soft, the skull acquired the desired flattened shape within a few days, This deformation gave them an air for dignity and valour. The forehead no longer juted out in such a way that *Ik*, the God of the Wind, could throw himself against it as against a wall but had instead acquired a smooth, sloping surface along which the wind could pass without hinderance and which directly received the sun.

According to these aesthetic precepts, to be cross-eyed was considered the height of elegance. Hence, some mothers hung a colourful bead close to the eyes of their children in their cradles so that, by looking at it and following its swinging with their eyes, the children became cross-eyed.

Both men and women decorated their teeth with insets of jade and obsidian and sometimes filed them into points. Both sexes pierced their ears in order to be able to wear ear rings. However, only the warriors pierced their lower lip and nostril in which they inserted rings.

The function of body painting was not only decorative but also magical. The different colours represented forces and vibrations. The application of certain colours on the body imbued it with specific forces and for this reason body painting was practiced especially in religious or war-time activities. The coloured soils were applied with resins. The youths painted themselves black. Blue was used for sacrificial rites and other major ceremonies and was exclusive to the priests. The warriors painted their bodies red and black because these colours were considered to be in conflict, opposing and dialectic. They were also related to wisdom and were used during fasts and penitence. The women never coloured their faces although they did paint their breasts, shoulders and arms and to the mixture was added a little *itz-tahté*, which was a strongly perfumed resin which had the property of making them pleasant and attractive.

Of greater importance than body painting was the practise of tattooing. It was, nevertheless, not as common as body painting because it was permittted only for those of lineage, hierarchy, outstanding bravery or other valid motives since its function was to emphasize the identity. Hence, city crests were drawn on the skin in the case, for example, of an important marriage between two persons from different places; or the name; or signs symbolizing an event; or totemic and protecting animals such as the jaguar, the snake or prized birds.

The hair was dressed and cared for with great attention since it was believed that it was in the hair that the force of life accumulated. It was related to anything undulating such as the spirits of the wind and the rivers and with the mysterious sinuousness of the serpent.

The women's hair, always clean and shining with health-giving oils, was parted in the centre and worn in coils, like serpents, covering part of the ears. There were variations on this style, consisting sometimes of a single coil or of four points which was the manner most often adopted by young girls. The men, however, cut or singed the hair on the crown of the head leaving only a lock on the forehead which was tied with a ribbon to hold it erect while the rest of the hair fell loose over the shoulders or was wound around the head leaving a pigtail. Perhaps in a desire to imitate the crests of birds which lend them their elegance, they always sought to use their hair as a means of heightening their gracefulness.

Headdresses were also used to increase their air of elegance but these were exclusive to important personages and priests since they were a means of identifying rank. There were many varied designs, each corresponding to a different level of the hierarchy. Spectacular plumes were implanted in a framework of willow covered with jaguar, snake or deer skin. The brilliantly coloured feathers could be arranged either in a rigid crest or in a fan or, alternatively, cascading down over the back of the head.

The attire of the major lords was truly astonishing. They were accustomed to adorning themselves with necklaces, bracelets, noserings, earrings, anklets and knee chains all of which were fashioned from valuable materials such as jade and precious feathers, obsidian, shells, teeth and jaguar claws. The ordinary people wore more simple decorations such as rings, earrings, nose and lip rings of bone, wood and other materials of little value.

Their clothing was simple, elegant and, above all, comfortable. The men wore an *ex,* a type of loin cloth which was colourfully embroidered in the case of dignitaries who also wore a brightly coloured sleeveless jacket decorated with embroidery and feathers called a *xicul.* They further wore the *suyen,* a square mantle which passed under the right arm and was knotted on the left shoulder. The women dessed in a square smock with a *pic* or underskirt showing below it. Their sandals, called *xanab,* were either of deer hide or agave fibres and these were also decorated in accordance with social standing.

Children generally went barefoot for the first years of their lives. The young women were given a red shell attached to a cord which hung from the belt and covered their sex as a symbol of their virginity. The young men wore a white bead attached to the hair on the crown of the head.

"*A headdress was worn to give a heightened appearance of charm and elegance, this practice being reserved for those of rank...*"

The hetzmek ceremony

Cuzam was, very happy because Keh had reached four months of age and the time had come to celebrate the *hetzmek* which meant that she could carry the child for the first time astride her hip. After enjoying a leisurely bath she dressed for the festivities. The courtyard smelt of damp earth and a great quantity of maize pancakes or *tortillas* and other foods which she had prepared early that morning were laid out next to the hearth. Cuzam gazed at the hearth and thought of the fact that if her child had been a girl the ceremony would have taken place a month earlier in accordance with the custom. In the case of a girl, the festivities were held three months after the child was born on account of the three stones of the hearth, the symbol of womanly tasks. On the other hand, for the boys, the four months symbolized the corners of the field for sowing which was related to male tasks.

Ah Otz was chosen as godfather since he had shown them great affection for many years. It was important to choose the godfather with care because he played an important part in the infant's upbringing. Ah Otz was a merchant and, in recognition of his intelligence and seemly conduct, the was often given the job of ambassador, carrying important messages between different cities. Ah Tzab chose him as godfather bearing in mind that it would be very instructive for his son to be able to accompany the ambassador on his travels.

When the sun had risen high enough in the sky the guests began to arrive. They formed into small groups and lively conversation was to be heard all around. Dialogue was very important to these people. It allowed the thoughts and experiences of others to be communicated. They enjoyed meeting together to discuss events in the city and each spoke of his own activities. Therefore, comments were to be heard such as: "I received a large guantily of splendid jade and I have already begun to carve a plaque to commemorate the ascension of *Halach uinic* to the throne"; "The astronomers have announced that there will soon be another eclipse, the jaguar will again sink his teeth into the sun"; "The date is approaching when one of the Xiu lords, from Uxmal, will come to the city to compete in the sacred game of pelota. It will be a sumptuous ceremony"; and, a little removed, the old men in whispers solemnly discussed the sad presages threatening the town.

When most of the guests had arrived the ceremony began. A table was placed in the centre of the courtyard and on this Ah Otz laid out nine objects connected to the vocation of his godson: a sheet of amate paper, a little clay, a particle of a mineral producing a yellow dye, wood charcol, a bag of *pom,* a brush of feathers, a hair painthbrush, a seal and a table of hierogliphics. All these articles related to the tasks of a codex painter were considered as valued objects, especially by those attending the ceremony and they were further regarded as sacred objects.

Ah Tzab handed the child to his godfather who took him lovingly in his arms and placed him astride his left hip. Then he walked around the table, picking up each of the articles in turn and giving them to the child as he explained their function. This was a public confirmation of the fact that the young Keh would receive a thorough artistic and historical education. He would acquire great knowledge of how time passed and how to record it and of the symbols to narrate events and facts. Furthermore, the *hetzmek* ceremony served to emphasize the child's identily as a male.

Having walked several more times around the table, this time with a religious significance connected with the *Bolontikú* the Lords of the Night, telling the child that all men are mortal and, before dying, should execute their duties in life, Ah Otz handed the child back to his parents and pronounced the following words with great emotion: "Your son has received the *hetzmek,* his obligations are confirmed". Cutzam and Th Tzab tooc back their child and knelt before the godfather as a gesture of gratitude. Shortly afterwards, all partook of the food and drink.

Infancy

During the first four years of life, children were given great freedom. They were allowed to grow up much as puppies, receiving essential attention such as love, nourishment and bathing. The children were never drawn into adult troubles and worries. They were not subject to any discipline but since children are naturally inclined to imitate their elders, parents were very careful in the way they behaved and paid attention to their personal image so that the children should have before them an example worthy of being followed. The paragdym was the secret of early training.

Cuzam and Ah Tzab were as aware as any other parents that in play children develop their bodies and their minds. What appears to be merely amusement is in fact the child's expression of reality. Imagination, inventiveness and creative ability blossom in play. Like other children, Kek wondered naked all day. His bare feet were agile for running and climbing. Nobody sought to prevent him from climbing trees or the stone wall around his house. On the contrary, he was encouraged to discover the possibilities of his body, his agility; to reap enjoyment from the landscape, the climate, nature and space. He was not punished from any clumsiness or errors but was shown rather by example how he should behave. He received basic teaching in music, dance and singing that he might learn to express himself without constraint. Even at such an early age he had already learnt to perforate a reed to fashion a flute and to stretch a hide over a gourd to make a drum. He was free to make friends and play with groups of children since this was a basis for learning to live in a community and relate socially.

His parents did, however, take great care in teaching him habits of cleanliness and hygiene. Cuzam bathed Keh every day in the courtyard in a wooden tub filled with water warmed by the sun. Sometimes at night, when the child had got very dirty playing, Cuzam would heat water over the hearth and the child would be bathed a second time. Sometimes he was taken along to the steam baths. These were clay domes built over a hollow in the earth which contained heated stones giving off steam when water was thrown over them. Keh watched this whole process and saw how the steam was released through holes high up in the walls. The bathers rubbed their bodies with herbs which served to speed up the circulation of the blood and produce a feeling of relaxation and well being. Some of these herbs were medicinal, a great variety being used, depending on the illness being treated. The steam bath was also an act of purification, giving rise to the songs and prayers which rid the bather

"*Keh would never forget the day he was taken to visit the precious bird aviary...*"

of impurities of the body and soul. These baths were large enough to accomodate a whole family at once and a person skilled in medecine and the purification ritual was generally in attendance. There were also large public baths were whole families waited their turn in cubicles.

Outings were also an integral part of a child's early education. Keh would never forget the days on which he was taken to see the aviaries of precious birds. In a huge area filled with trees and plants, protected by an enormous net of agave fibre, these birds were bred in order to obtain the feathers which fell when they molted. These were then used in feather art. Birds were sacred to the Mayas since in their song could be heard the voices of the gods and their plumage was one of the most highly prized natural objets used to identify those men such as priests and dignitaries who were intermediaries between the people and the gods. As a result of the care taken by the Mayas to preserve the different species, there were birds of many different plumages. In accordance with their hue and brilliant shine, some were propitious for war, others for sowing and trade and the most beautiful had power to gratify the gods who, from their different seats, looked on when members of the hierarchy, as well as musicians and dancers, adorned themselves with impressive feather headdresses for their ceremonies which were a display of beauty in honour of the gods.

Keh examined the birds with astonishment and listened delighted to their song. Glimpses of feathers as red as embers shone out from among the greens of the foliage and An Tzab explained to his son that these were solar birds and for this reason they glowed like fire; orange and yellow had similar attributes. Green plumages mingled with the leaves and others of brilliant blue streaked with phosphorescent green brought to mind the sparkle of swiftly flowing water. There were brown and black birds and others of dappled plumage and yet more of contrasting colours and of snowy white.

When Keh had had his fill of this enchantment, Ah Tzab took him to the feather art workshop. It was a long hall where dozens of craftsmen concentrated on their work. An astonishing variety of feathers were heaped on the floor. The craftsmen, seated on low wooden stools, arranged the feathers on backings of cloth, leather or willow frames. Some stuck the feathers down with resin while others sewed them with hemp twine. And the feathers came together to form plumes, headpieces, shields, breastplates, bracelets, knee chains and cloaks. They skillfully interwove zoomorphic borders and figures. On some articles of clothing, a fringe of feathers was added and great attention was paid to the combination of colours. But these were not the only articles they fashioned. Other craftsmen were engaged in creating marvellous fans, earrings and necklaces. Feathers were also attached to lances and arrows in such a way that they seemed as birds when they flew through the air. Sceptres were also embellished in this way. Keh wondered whether it would be possible to fly using artificial wings because he grasped the fact that there are two elements inherent in feathers, that of beauty and that of flight.

One morning, Ah Tzab found Keh fashioning clay figures. The child had stuck feathers from the birds they raised in the yard into the head of one of the statuettes. Tzab smiled and decided that it was time he took his son to see the potters at work. Their workshop consisted of three halls and a large courtyard. Several men were working on the *kabal*, a square wooden board which was revolved with the foot. This left the hands free to mould the clay and soon the shapeless mass began to take form, acquired a neck, a more defined shape as a cup or vase of either spherical or cylindrical form. Other potters beat clay into rolls on wooden boards then placed them upright and carved the clay into human or animal form with pieces of sharpened shell. Such was their skill that gradually faces, arms, legs, heads or claws appeared and the figures were so lifelike that it seemed they could really see and that they would begin to move at any moment. Some were individual statuettes but others combined to form interesting groups of dancers, warriors or hunters or women balancing baskets on their heads on the way to the market, or giving the breast to their infants or making tortillas. Keh saw in these life-like figures a representation of life as it was in his town as though the reason for these works was to depict everyday life as a testimony to all that the life of man implied in the activity of the universe.

"They make clay lie", warned Tzab, "they make it change and feign to be what it is not". In astonishment Keh followed the movements of the hand of a potter fashioning a jaguar. "He is fashioning a god"; his father explained to him. The jaws were so ferocious and the muscles as though tensed to leap, the beast was so vigorous, so magnificent that any beholder was immediately struck by an awareness of a divine presence.

The decoraters worked in another hall on truncks of *kuché* or red cedar which had been planed down to produce a flat surface. All types of vessels and figures were ranged along the work benches and were being coloured with painstaking precison. Here the artists worked much more slowly; the paint brushes were dipped into shells containing a mixture of dyes and resins and was applied with upmost accuracy to the clay as though it was being imbued with life. These artists were in fact masters in chromogenic science, knowing how to produce exactly the colour they desired. Keh could see many household articles which were in great demand in the markets as well as those of a ceremonial nature upon which the artists demonstrated their most consumate skills although the child was still too young to understand the significance of the designs. Highly significant messages were inscribed on the vessels in accordance with their function either as offerings to the gods or as funereal, votive objects. Before assuming the task of painting the codices, Keh would be engaged for a time in this workshop in order to develop his drawing ability and to learn the significance of signs and symbols which were understood only by scholars and wise men of the community.

Outside in the courtyard were to be seen the objects for sale and these amply demonstrated the care taken by the artists, imbuing each object with love and spirit. The fact that they were destined for daily use did not obviate delicateness and beauty. The oven for baking the clay was situated close at hand. Dozens of images of the godess Ixchel were being taken from the flaming mouth of one of the ovens as they approached. The statues were bright red in colour, so much so that they seemed a more accurate representation of the sun deity than of the moon godess. Lying there on the ground they seemed to have been ejected from a flaming womb with the ability to produce gods by the dozen that they might come to earth to satisfy all human needs. Ixchel, from her place in the heavens, must have been moved to see that man sought her and reproduced her image in orden to venerate her.

The age of discipline and polishing

After these four initial years of total freedom, another phase of the child's life began. He was now subjected to a certain discipline and given responsabilities. Outings were designed to promote a full awareness of the duties of the individual. For this reason, Keh now began to spend short periods, some two or three days, in the company of farmers and hunters. In this way he became aware that the economy of the city depended to a large extent on the work of these people who provided food for the population.

Keh was able to see how land was prepared for cultivation. During the winter an area of forest was cleared. Certain rites were then performed to make the land ready for sowing. In the four corners of the cleared area, which corresponded to the four corners of the universe, a priest buried seed, copal, jars of honey and clay statuettes depicting the gods of agriculture. The votive offerings would ensure that *Chaac* sent the rains which were the sole means of irrigation since artificial irrigation was impossible, given the rocky texture of the soil. Having thus ensured divine protection over the newly cleared land, when the uprocted undergrowth was sufficiently dry, some four or five months into the new year, the area was burned. The land was then ready for planting some two months later when the rains began. The seeds were planted with a *xul,* a rod with a pointed, firehardened tip. This instrument served to make holes in the bottom of the furrows, each hole accomodating several grains of maize mixed with a marrow seed or two and a few black beans. The seed beds were weeded regularly to allow the plants to develop freely. By the ninth month young, tender maize was ready for harvesting. The next step was to drain the seed beds to protect them from damp and to allow the ears of maize to harden. When the time was right, the maize was harvested and distributed in accordance with immediate needs and the remainder stored in a granery in the fields. A plot of land was used for three or four consecutive years but the yield dropped with each consecutive planting and therefore it was necessary to periodically clear new land, following the same procedure. When a plot had laid fallow for some seven years it was agair sufficiently fertile for planting. The organic loss caused by the burning of the newly cleared areas was indeed tragic and often the farmers were forced to move further and further afield right into the mountains to find new land. Maize was the major crop since it was a staple part of the Mayan diet and was, moreover, considered to be divine.

Two types of black bean were also grown; the *xcolibul*

and the *tzamá* as well as *itz,* sweet potato; *chicam,* an type of edible plant; *macal* and *macalbox,* types of roots; *ic,* chili; *chay,* chaya vegetable; *p'tc,* tomato; *kum* and *xcá,* marrow; *kiixpaxhkum,* chayote; *kikitzin,* yuca, and others.

Other men cultivated orchards and *Keh* became familiar with plantations of *on,* advocado pear; *ya,* sapodilla; *op,* plums; *dzamul,* sayamuyo fruit; *put,* papaya; *chi,* nance and *tauch,* the marmalade tree. To the east lay luxuriant plantations of cacao of which the seeds, besides being edible, served as currency. Hence, Keh was able to learn that nature's gifts were rich but that man had to work if he was to make the land produce and not leave it barren. Fruit was the delight of children, to see them glowing in the trees and to savour their different flavours. "The gods feed us", said Ah Tzab, "they give us delicious fruits to strengthen our blood and our bodies. Therefore we should be grateful to the gods who give us sustenance".

Different types of trees grew in other parts of the hills. Some produced gourds which could be used as containers and the inner fibre of others served to fashion sandals and other necessary articles. Of course the most highly prized woods were *kuché,* red cedar; that of the *yá,* the marmalade tree and that of the *kikché* which was admirably suited to the construction of canoes. Keh greatly admired the way in which the truck was hollowed out on the ground and gazing at the clouds sailing over rivers and seas, driven by up to thirty oarsmen, depending on the length of the trunk.

Keh said to his father, "I want to travel along the roads which move", which was his way of describing rivers and, referring to the sea he said, "I want to travel over the waters which are as wide as the heavens". Ah

"*Deer, like pheasant, was killed only
to provide food for the high-ranking officials
who consumed it ritually in ceremonies. . .*"

Tzab explained to him that these were hard and danger-
ous journeys and that for this reason young children
were rarely taken along. However, his father assured
him that he would soon be old enough to accompany
his godfather Ah Otz on his business trips. Stretched
out on the ground and gazing at the clouds sailing over the
crests of the trees, Keh conjured up the marvellous experiences of "those of the light feet" or the merchants
who travelled long distances on overland roads. Or better still, the exciting adventures of the travellers "who
journied on wood along the moving roads, the sailors of
the time. The roll of a drum awoke him abruptly from
his daydreams. And the fact was that not only canoes
but also *tunkules* and others objets were constructed
in the region. Everybody, even the children, joined in
the production of washtubs, wooden jars and numerous
other utensils. Some cut branches from a tree of soft,
light coloured wood for use as rollers to transport huge
blocks of stone which were brought to the city from far
afield for use in building. The voices, the sweating men,
the sawing of wood all created an impression of hard
work.

Keh, on several occasions, had the opportunity to accompany other children to the fields of *taman* or cotton
to gather the white silky tufts it produced. Cotton was
the most highly prized plant for fabric since most clothing was made of this material. Other valuable fibres were
those of the silk-cotton tree, called *choo, piim* and *po-
chote*. *Ki* or sisal was also cultivated, the fibres being
obtained by scraping the leaves with wooden instruments
known by the name of *toncoz ché* and *pac ché*. This
process produced a pungent odour and the air appeared
to be filled with a warm vapour. Aware that it would be

interesting for the child, Ah Tzab showed him the plants producing the dyes used both for dying cotton and for body painting and tattooing. Among such plants was the *ek,* dye plant; *ch'oh,* indigo and *k'uxab* of the annatto tree. Keh asked whether these were the dyes used in codex painting. He was told that this was indeed the case but that, in codex painting, the dyes were mixed with resins and he was further given details about the many different coloured soils and of sea conch dye which, he was told, was highly recommended.

The child was rarely allowed to join in hunting expeditions. Keh was somewhat clumsy with the cross bow and the lance but, nevertheless, he found it a very interesting experience. Hunting took place either in the early morning or at night fall or even at the dead of night. The hunters brought home a wide variety of game which had been killed either in traps or with arrows, darts or javelins, including such animals as the *Keh* (deer), the *kitam* (wild boar), *jaleb* (paca), *thul* (rabbit) and the *uech* (armadillo). Dogs called *ahkehpek* were used in the hunting of deer because they had an extraordinary sense of smell and could follow any scent and they were, furthermore, fast runners. Like pheasant, venison was eaten only by the high dignitaries and then only as a ritual during ceremonies. Venison was on no account a food of the people whose diet consisted chiefly of *cutz* (wild turkey) or *tzo* (domestic turkey); edible, hairless dogs called *bil* and *cutzha* or duck and other animals such as turtles from the fresh water springs and iguanas which lived in cracks of the limestone rock.

After his first hunting expedition, Keh attended a ceremony which made a great impression on him. Since the hunt had been poor, the idols in a sanctuary on the far side of the mountain were whipped and insulted. "Why do they insult the gods?" asked Keh in astonishmet, "surely the gods should be teated with reverence". He was given to understand that there were lesser gods who served the great ones. Those who were being punished were merely assistants who had rendered poor service and were being treated in this way to encourage them to do better in the future. However, after Keh's second hunt, which had been very fruitful, the subsequent ceremony took a different form. Blood from the carcasses was annointed on the faces of the images of the greater gods in a gesture of honour. The ceremony was repeated nine times before the gods and seven times before the godesses. In this way, the gods were simultaneously venerated and given sustenance. After a good hunt, the lesser divinities also received a little blood and, on occasions, songs of gratitude. After the ceremony, the game was divided. The victorius hunters ware entitled to the heads, legs and kidneys and the remainder of the meat was shared out among the rest of the hunters of expedition. Certain cuts were also set aside for the *batabes*, the priests and high officials.

Keh dreamed of going to the sea and living with the fishermen but, since the opportunity did not arise, he was not to have his way. However, since he was so interested, he was shown the instruments used in this activity: nets, hooks, harpoons, arrows and bows. He was taken to the market to watch the delivery of large quantities of salted fish which had been dried in the sun to preserve it. Large quantities had to brought to the city because the white, nourishing flesh was greatly appreciated by the people.

All these activities were designed to teach the child

the value of work. He had been allowed to take part in order to teach him to respect those engaged in these different professions rather than to become highly skilled in each and every one of them. This served to develop his sensitivity to the things and activities taking place around him, that he might better fulfill the aesthetic and moral standards that constituted the foundation of that society. Observation of the work of others was an integral part of discipline and learning and, as children grew up, they were introduced to ever more complex notions and they were subjected to increasingly severe discipline. So, while young children were free from all discipline or punishment, from the age of four onwards they were expected to shoulder responsabilities and were severely punished for their shortcomings.

One day Keh and his friends were playing in a *kiixpachkum* plantation and, carried away by their game, they picked several chayotes to kick and throw like a ball. Their parents made them fast for three days and belabour their thighs with blows before the gods of agriculture in penitence and repentence. And their punishment was more severe still when the children were caught killing birds with a pea-shooter since this was considered to be very cruel and it was strictly forbidden to kill animals merely for amusement. Ah Tzab rebuked his son, "Never, never pick a fruit when you are not in need of food and it is worse still to kill an animal withhout reason or justification". As punishment for his misbehaviour, Keh fasted for five days and again did penitence before the gods of agriculture. When Keh laughed at the sight of an old lady who fell down in the market place, Cuzam immediately took him home and made him stand over a dish of toasting chilis until the smoke made tears pour from his eyes. This was a punishment normally reserved for girls and Keh was overcome with shame.

If a child repeated a misdemeanour for which he had already been chastised, he was warned and again punished on occasions. However, if he failed to heed his elders' word and abide by the rules which they laid down, if he ignored laws and duties or showed signs of indifference or rebelliousness, then more drastic measures were taken to correct his inclinations and strengthen his will. These meausures aimed to correct a child's behaviour and which were often more painful to the parents than to the children themselves were designed to polisch children who had reached the age in which baits are formed.

Keh would not soon forget the punishments he had suffered and therefore was more inclined to think twice before acting and paid heed to his parents warnings in order to avoid falling into error. He watched his parents and imitated their behaviour. He was fully aware that theft, lack of respect and disobedience would prevent him from developing a noble heart and dignified aspect. It was clear by then that, through his parents guidance, Keh had learned to aspire to perfection.

"*The sun will indeed rise, his mother replied,
and you will witness the descent of God
and you will live a long life to fulfill
your duties. . .*"

The descent of god

After carefully consulting the calendar, Ah Tzab selected a suitable day for the ceremony to celebrate his son's reaching the age of puberty. On this occasion, Keh would be given due warnings for his transition from adolescence to adulthood. Ah Tzab then arranged with other parents to hold a joint ceremony for all the boys and girls who were of a suitable age.

Keh spent a sleepless night on account of his excitment and the thoughts going through his head and got up before the sun rose. Cuzam was already busy at her daily early morning task of preparing maize pancakes or tortillas at the hearth. "Will *Kin* rise today?" the boy asked her, his young voice betraying the uncertainty of one who fears that the sun will not appear and that there will be no new day, bringing the end of all things. 'It will rise", his mother answered him, "and you will feel god descend upon you. You will live long to fulfill your duties". His mother's voice inspired confidence and he seated himself beside her and drank a preparation sweetened with honey. At Cuzam's suggestion he went out into the courtyard to drink in the early light of the new day. Kin, the sun, rose victorious and brightnees fell upon the earth and all things trembled. He reflected upon the event for a few minutes and then bathed himsef in cold water. He impatiently awaited the return of his father who had spent the night in one of the temples. Some hours later, the three walked slowly along the white road which crossed the city of Chichén Itzá until they reached the dwellings of the high dignitaries, the buildings standing together in perfect harmony. They were solidly buit, with beautiful lintles of wood and sculptured door jambs. Several adolescents, in the company of their parents, had already gathered in the rectangular patio which was flanked by other buildings. The girls stood together in a group and the boys in another. Keh joined his companions. The whole area was carpeted with green leaves which were pleasant to the feet. The air was charged with excitment when the priest appeared in the company of four *chaques,* his assistants and the godparents of the young people. The priest carried a hyssop of carved wood with rattle snake tails hanging from it. Any movement of the hyssop produced a rattle which frightened off evil spirits and drought. The priest moved right round the patio to clear it of harmful spirits. Once the area had been thus purified, the assitants dampened the leaves underfoot with water from the sacred spring. At once the air seemed to become lighter, it was easier to breath and the humid green carpet attracted *Chaac,* the god of the jade countenance. All present were aware of a feeling that the place was protected. The priest then changed his robes, appearing in a cloak embroidered with yellow feathers with a green plume upon his head. A straw mat was placed in the centre of the patio and the *chaques* seated themselves upon it, one in each corner. The godparents stepped forward, one a high dignitary who, besides acting as godfather to the males, also paid for the festivity, and an old woman who was godmother to the girls. The *chaques* covered the children's heads with a white cloth and questioned them on their behaviour. Those who had misbehaved were separated from the group. All sat in absolute silence as the priest sprinkled them with sacred water and intoned praises. The godparents touched the forehead of each child nine times with a fragment of bone and them proceeded to annointed their faces, the spaces between their fingers and between their toes. The priests then removed the white cloths from their heads and the children presented their offerings. The gifts met with approval and were accepted as a sign that the children had acquired new responsabilitites in the community. This was the moment when the priest cut the white beads from the males' hair and the mothers removed the red shell from the belts of their daughters as a sign that they were of an age to marry. The *chaques* lit enormous pipes and blew huge clouds of smoke to purify the young bodies. The boys were given a vessel filled with *balché* of which they took a sip and gave the remainder to the *chaques* who drank it without pausing for breath. In a line, the young people entered the building to meditate while the parents remained outside to exchange gifts of feathers and blankets and commence the festivities with food and drink. Only the godparents refrained from partaking since, not only had they fasted for three days previously, but they would continue to do so for a further nine days in penitence for having induced the descent of god.

It was already late when the family returned home. Ah Tzab gave Keh his first loin cloth and a pair of sandals. He would no longer be able to go around naked and would have to spend many days in a communal building for young men where he would engage in sports such as pelota, running, javelin throwing and he would be taught to dance and sing. This would be his principle place of learning.

The gods

Each day, the teachers conducted classes in the building in which the young men were lodged. A knowledge of the attributes of the gods, their powers and their spheres of action was of great importance. A day arrived upon which Keh had to take an examination in front of one of the priests, Ah Kin Tzoc, to show how far he had progressed in his knowledge of the divinities. The exam was to take place at midnight. Keh had nothing to fear because any error or ignorance would merely show that he needed further study. He had fasted for three days beforehand and had pierced his tongue with the spike of the agave plant in order to attain a state of purity and be fit to pronounce the names of the gods.

Keh waited all evening outside the priest's house. He wached *Kin* sink into the entrails of the underworld. The red light had faded from tre sky and the first stars came out. Standing there, he exercised his mind and allowed divine inspiration to seep into him. The soft, maternal moon had swung in her orbit until she reached the highest point in the sky and seemed to bathe the magnificent buildings of the city with her glow. A conch sounded the hour of his examination. Keh climbed a narrow stairway and reached a door where two men were waiting for him. They led him into the presence of Ah Kin Tzoc who awaited him in a large courtyard on the south side of the building. The night was tranquil and the pair would stroll back and forth across the large open courtyard as the boy answered the questions asked by the priest.

"Who is the godess of the Cord?" the old man asked him. "She is called *Ixtab*", replied Keh, "she hangs from the heavens from a cord tied around her neck. Her symbol is a cord and also the silk-cotton tree which is sacred. *Ixtab's* eyes are closed in death and a black circle is inscribed on one of her cheeks, symbolizing the decomposition of the flesh. Those who renounce life by hanging themselves from a silk-cotton tree will attain paradise. Eternal lodging in divine regions is the reward of those who end their lives at their own hand in penitence for pleasure and nourishment.

The old man corrected nothing, added nothing but when they walked through a patch of light he asked:

"Who was your first protecting divinity?"

"Ixcel", the boy replied with gladness, "because she is the godess of pregnancy and birth and protects those who are about to be born. She is the godess of everything female, she invented weaving, spinning and the art of making clothing. It is she who forms our features in the maternal womb and by her that life is born. She brings about the ebb and flow of the tide".

"So she must be all goodness", inquired the old man.

"She is also godess of the floods. Her symbols are those of destruction and death. In her skirt she carries two crossed bones and on her head a serpent coil. She is water which destroys and causes the end of things. She unleashes torrents of rain and created the flood which put an end to an era".

"So, she is to be feared. She is the godess of calamity!" suggested the priest.

"But not only feared", clarified Keh, "we have far more to be grateful to her for. For, if she is death, she is also life. Also, she is the companion of *Itzamná*".

"And... who is Itzamná?"

"The Lord of the Heavens", explained Keh, "son of *Hunab Ku,* creator of the beginning. He is represented by the sign for the day *Ahau,* the last and most important of the twenty days of the month. *Ahau* means Lord, ruler, emperor. Hence, *Itzamná* is a leader among the gods and presides over the society of the divinities. He is all creative, he never destroys and is therefore never associated with symbols of death. *"Itzamná* is indeed great", replied the old man, "and he is of course brother of *Kinich Ahau".*

"Oh, no", retorted Keh, *"Kinich Ahau,* Lord of the Eye of the Sun, is Itzamná himself, it is one of his manifestations as Lord of the Day. *Itzamná* controls *Ixchel,* his wife, and when he counsels her the waters are calm and safe to travel. In the month of *Zip* they are both considered to be God of Medecine because, when their names are invoked, sickness disappears. When he is not heedful, epidemics break out on the earth."

The youth and the old man walk to and fro across the courtyard. They trod slowly as though this opened

"And... who is Itzamná? The Lord of the
Skies, explained Keh, son of Hunab Ku,
creator of the beginning. Of Itzamná is born
the day and the night..."

the mind to a clearer understanding of things. In one corner, a perfectly worked projection of stone jutted from an arris. The priest gazed at it and asked the boy:

"Who is this god?"

"Chaac", answered Keh with a shudder of pleasure in pronouncing the name. "He is the God of Rain. His generosity is to be seen in his long nose and jagged teeth. One eye contains the representation of a tear which refers to the rain which he sends. He is the god of fertility because it is he who nourishes the earth. His bounty fills the wells with water and his wrath leaves them dry. He is four gods in one and each of his parts occupies one of the four cardinal points: *Chac Xib Chaac* is the Red Man of the East; *Sax Xib Chaac* is the White Man the North; *Ek Xib Chaac* is the Black Man of the West and *Kan Xib Chaac* is the Yellow Man of the South. *Ik,* the God of the Wind, is his companion and they work together. It is *Ik* who causes the clouds to move to the places selected by *Chaac* that rain might fall there. Man is in great need of their friendly intervention because our livlihood depends upon it.

"Only on *Chaac* and *Ik,* his helper?"

"No indeed", replied Keh. "The entire universe is sustained by all the gods. If we are talking about the food which men eat, we must not forget the God of Maize whose name is not spoken. We are dependent on many other gods besides. I could also mention the spirits which live in the *Ak'Al,* the marsh where water abounds and those who accompany the *Bacaboob,* Those who spread Water who together constitute a single god called *Ah Cantzicnal Bacab,* the Bringer of Water to the Four Corners, who is responsible for the *Hahal,* the rainy season. *Hahal K'u,* the True Deity is also important as is *Ix Chuah,* the One who Fills. *Ah K'inchil,* the Sun's Face, shines down to bring greenness to the plants and our mountains are protected by the *Ahkanankaxob,* whose greatest Lord is *Yum Kax,* God of Maize who grants us prosperity and plenty.

"Great should be our gratitude since there are so many who nurture us", the old man advised him. He then asked:

"What do you know of the *Bacaboob?"*

"They are four in number and have four hundred thousand manifestations in accordance with their activities. I have already mentioned one such manifestation as Those who Spread Water: another is as Sustainers of the Sky and another as Sustainers of the Earth. *Bacaboob* are also those who carry conch and turtle shells and the *Ah Muzencaboob,* related to the *uayeb* days, five extra days in the year which are not accounted for. For this reason they represent old age, the termination, the return to chaos. At times they manifest themselves as gods who fertilize flowers and then they are called *Zec,* lords of the beehives".

"Who is honoured by the cacao growers?".

"Hobnil and more especially *Ek Chuah".*

"Who protects merchants and travellers?"

"Xaman Ek, God of the Polar Star. Unlike *Chaac,* he has a hooked nose and dark marks upon his cheek by which we know that he is a heavenly being and shines in the darkness. He is always visible in the night to guide travellers on their way. He is a good god because he illuminates the road and dispels uncertainty at the crossroads".

"And who is the one who also shines in the night but awakes our fears?"

"Noth Ek, the planet Venus. When *Kin* sheds his brightest light upon us, *Noh Ek* falls headfirst into hell. There he engages daily in combat with the shadows and, although he overcomes them, he rises at night contaminated with evil forces which we should not contemplate but they diominish in strength as his glow grows brighter. By midnight the evil forces are totally dispelled and *Noh Ek* is purified and becomes benevolent".

"What is the name of the god who crawls and flies?"

"Kukulcan, tre Plumed Serpent. He is the dual god, he is both flesh and spirit, the earth which aspires to the heavens and the heavens which descend to earth, he is good and evil, black and white, the ethereal and the concrete, sound and silence. Chaos finds harmony in him because he is *Kukulcan,* the meeting of opposites."

"Which is the god whose eye is partially surrounded by a black line which continues down his cheek?"

"Ek Chuah, the god of two faces, one benevolent and one manevolent. He is not only god of cocao but also God of War and violent death, he who burns houses and hearts with a flaming torch. It is he who, with the help of *Ik,* directs the course of arrows. He boosts bravery and courage and dispells fear from the hearth. He is the God of Sacrifice and the God of Death is his companion."

"Who is the God of Death and where is he to be found?"

His name is *Ah Puch* and he is also called *Yum Kimil* and he is at once in the heavens and in the underworld".

"Who else inhabits the underworld?"

"The god Jaguar who is the sun on its nightly journey. Also the *Bolontikú,* the Lords of the Night".

"Into how many parts are the heavens and the underworld divided and which part does each god inhabit?".

Keh was assailed by doubt in answering this question, his mind could not embrace and comprehend the dimensions of the universe. The priest affectionately stroked the child's cheek and lifted him up that he might contemplate the profundity of the heavens.

"The heavens are divided into thirteen parts", the old man explained in a hushed voice. "It has thirteen regions and the *Oxlahuntikú*, the heavenly gods, are distributed among these regions. A great silk-cotton tree stretches across the centre of the earth, burying its roots deep into the underworld and raising its branches to the heavens. The gods use the tree to ascend and descend and, since they are omnipresent, they can be simultaneously on earth, in the metnal, or underworld and in the heavens. The gods are many faceted and change in both appearance and dress, they may be good and evil, depending on whether they are pleased with man's behaviour and whether he has fulfilled the destiny marked out for him. Contemplate the stars and you will see the number of our Lords and Gods living on high. They are both there and, at the same time, here on earth. The gods from the underworld live in the depths yet they pillage our fields and cities".

"Are there many gods in the underworld?" Keh asked.

"Indeed, as many as in the heavens", answered the old man. "The gods of war and sacrifice live at the first gate and often act as leaders. *Cit Bolon Ua* lives further down. He is the Decider of Lies, he who deceives and his evil pranks lead others to follow him, in the manner of the opossum. Further into the depths we find *Ah Cup Cacap,* the one who suffocates us and deprives us of air. Another region is inhabited by *Uuc Stay,* he who is divided into seven forces of death, ever rapid and sudden. *Chac Bolay Can,* the crual red serpent frequents the darkest, deepest passages as do the bat and the owl which are symbols of death. We have hundreds upon hundreds of gods and all are magnificent! They are the masters of order which is why their activities are distributed among them and their hierarchy is solidly established. The lesser gods pay hommage to their superiors and when conflict arises among them, chaos reigs upon the earth.

Keh had successfully passed his examination. The priest turned upon the youth a face filled with satisfaction. They took leave of each other with great contentment. That night Keh was not to sleep in the communal dwelling of the young men. Ah Tzab awaited him outside to take him back to the family home. This separation from the other youths was designed to place him in an environment where he would be able to reflect and meditate. Keh felt the divine presence in his heart and he realized that there was no solitude because all space was inhabited by deities.

His mind dwelt on the gods as he prepared to sleep but, no sooner had he become drowsy, than Cuzam groaned. Ah Tzab got up to take care of her. "It is merely tiredness", she assured him, but pain and weakness plainly showed upon her face. As soon as it was light, Ah Tzab and Keh took her to see the doctor. He had the full confidence of all the inhabitants. He had knowledge of all the properties of medicinal herbs. He was well versed in the art of medicine and the gods looked kindly on him, so much so that he had once successfully opened the skull of a sick person to remo-

"But there is something fascinating
about Mayapán. The whole town bubbles with
activity. The town is so populous, it
seems that it gives the seed of life..."

ve the sickness that dwelt there. The doctor briefly examined the suffering woman and then took the *Am,* the divining stone which had been blest in the temple of *Ixchel.* He passed the stone over her stomach and finally gave his diagnosis: "Pregnancy, nothing to-worry about".

Keh was delighted at the prospect of having a younger brother or sister. Ah Tzab was also pleased. The youth embraced his mother in congratulation and, when he felt the warmth of her body, his mind was filled with thoughts of the complexity, wonder and pain of life. His mind turned to the hundreds of gods watching over them and his heart trusted in *Ixchel,* the godess who protected his birth and whose protection his parents would now enlist for a second time.

First journey to Uxmal and Mayapán

Just before midnight, Ah Otz and Keh set out on the road through the *sacbé* leading to the city of Uxmal. Shortly before, they had rendered hammage to *Xaman Ek,* god of the polar star and hence their guide. The road was white, straight and clearly lit by the moon. Their muffled steps could be heard over the night-time murmur of the wind, the foliage and the whisperings of the insects.

"Pay good attention to the road you tread", Ah Otz advised him, "because when you die you will have to retrace each step of your way throughout life. In this way you will recall all that you have lived through and hence be able to judge your own conduct and you will speak to the gods of all that you did in your existence".

"Many will be the steps that you will have to retread

since you are a traveller", exclaimed Keh. "Indeed", replied his godfather, "I will have to wander far and wide to retrace them all". "Do you fear dying? enquired the youth. The old man's reply was filled with profound aspirations: "My only fear is that my life will not be intense. Its' lenght is of no interest to me, only its intensity. I dedicate all my efforts to being useful in life".

On his back, the merchant carried a bundle filled with pieces of worked gold and silver. Among them were two masks which were not only worked in the usual Mayan fashion but had also been cast, an art mastered only by the Mixtecs. Hence, they were rare, valuable pieces. On this occasion, Ah Otz was travelling as an ambassador and not as a merchant. He had been charged to carry these gifts to the Lords of Uxmal and Mayapan in order to strengthen their relations with his own city of Chichén Itzá. Prophecies announcing the breakdown of their alliance had given rise to great anxiety and both the leaders and the people sought to ensure harmony and unity betweed the cities. However, as they continued along their way, Ah Otz wondered: "How can this disaster possibly be avoided if it has already been reflected in our sacred waters and been revealed to our visionaries and prophets?".

"Will we rest anywhere along the way?" Keh's question distracted Otz' mind from the thoughts which tortured him. Returning to the matter in hand, he paternally replied: "This road is neither long nor difficult so, in such cases, the traveller's best form of rest is to continue along the way at a steady pace. I have deliberately chosen to go slowly so as to conserve our stength and we are travelling by night out of the heat of the sun and the thirst it inflicts. You surely can't be tired?" he asked with surprise. "Certainly not", Keh staunchly replied, "I simply wished to know if travellers are provided with places to spend the night".

A look of pleasure suffused the old man's features as he cast his mind back over all the sactuaries placed at intervals along the long roads covered by the merchants. He recalled that there was always news from foreign parts to be learned in these places since the travellers spending the night in these santuaries came from far and wide. So, these places were a mine of information and messages were exchanged in order to save having to travel excessively long distances. The postal system fuctioned in the same way. The sanctuaries were welcoming and all sorts of services were provided. Food was to be had and the women washed the travellers' clothes and, on occasions, sales and exchanges were agreed upon. Travellers always Knew a great deal and that was what made their lives so interesting. They were as a figure of mosaic; the whole composed of many parts but seeming to belong to no single place but rather to arise from the immensity of space. They were loyal and true, ethically they could not lie since they were the bearers of news and information.

"When we go on longer journeys you will be introduced to these sanctuaries and you will have the opportunity and enjoyment of meeting all those who seek their hospitality. For the time being, on this journey, we will have reached a place where we will be given food by the time the sun rises and, from there, we have but a few hours journey before us to reach Uxmal".

Keh was overwhelmed by the city. Although some of the buildings were similar to those in Chichén Itzá with its Toltec architecture, this style certainly did not predominate. Serpent-shaped columns and other features which had been introduced in Chichén Itzá from Tula were here little in evidence. Keh marvelled at the grandeur of the buildings and open spaces. Soon a citizen of the city approached them, and was introduced to them as on of its most pretigious architects. Keh's godfather had taken pains to ensure that Keh's first journey was instructive and had arranged for this gentleman to explain the city to them. Hence, Keh learned that many of buildings which were familiar to him were in the *Puuc* style. This word meant: "land of the low hills" and so was used to designate the architecture of the calcareous area of Yucatán. The buildings of this style had smooth, undecorated walls topped with splendidly decorated friezes which were completed with cornices. A broad moulding surrounded the entire building. The design of the buildings gave a sense of harmony and the onlooker felt able to breath freely on account of the distribution of the wide, open spaces. Orthogonal buildings ran down both sides of the wide esplanades; the pyramids residing on mighty foundations appeared to rear their crests towards the regions of the gods. Their structure and majestic setting filled the beholder with wonder. The Mayan temples soared over the tree tops, man's handiwork excelling over nature. Keh shuddered with delight at these amazing achievements.

While Ah Otz went to deliver his gifts to the Lord of the *Xiu,* Keh's new friend took him to see the pyramid of the Prophet. The youth had never before set eyes on a building of such majesty combined with delicateness. Its rounded walls toned down the aggresiveness of the artists and lent it an air of nobility. The building seemed almost magical and that was why people claimed that it had been built by a being with supernatural powers, a dwarf hatched from an egg, the son of a sorceress. It was told that she had been condemned to death for her deeds and that she had persuaded the authorities to grant her pardon in exchange for which she would give them a building such as they had never before contemplated, even in the imagination. Night was falling as the dwarf placed the first stone and it was said that shortly afterwards all the citzens fell into a deep sleep as though bewitched. When they awoke the next morning, the place was covered in a blanket of vapour and mist. The mist was gradually blown away, revealing the magnificent building. This was how the event ocurred, to the astonishment of those who witnessed the marvel.

"Is this true?" asked Keh with amazement. "Of course not", replied the architect who took a great pride in his profession. "This tale is told because, as you must know, it is difficult to control flights of the imagination. It would appear that dreams and fantasies are the work of mischievous young gods who seek to divorce man from the reality of his existence".

When this was explained to him, Keh was overcome with embarrassment at having let himself be taken in by the legend. Then a fearful thought struck him, "Such is madness", he exclaimed, alarmed. "No indeed", his teacher explained, "it is simply fascinating distortion of reality. Man sometimes forgets that nature can hold its own fascination and turns to inventing, creating fiction, unfounded wonders. But this building is a reality created by human hand. Its heart is a natural outcrop of rock and its body is formed of a million tons of rock which cover and adorn the heart. Many were the men who brought loads of stone to the place. The work was arduous and exhausting but the very magnificence of the building shows the grandeur of the creative spirit of a people whose work has the power to impress the gods. Never have we sought to compete with their divine creations but simply to show them that we use the abilities they have granted us to their fullest possible extent".

They continued on their way, discussing the mathematical precision required in architecture and the way in which some of the buildings of the city faced points of astronomical interest. So they reached the Governor's Palace; the majesty of its architecture was immediately apparent. The decorative band low down on the wall of delicately worked mosaic. The perfectly hewn stones of 20 by 60 cm. were composed in such a way as to form a series of borders representing the serpent deity and a hundred and fifty masks of the god *Chaac*. All onlookers were struck by the immobile divine eyes which looked down upon them, by the curved fangs indicating the severity of the god and by the protruding noses which promised an abudance of rain. The frieze was made up of a total of 2,700 pieces. No error was to be seen in the arrangement. It seemed that perfection had been attained. Which was indeed the case, according to the architect who spoke with pride about the work of the store cutters, the sculpters and all those who participated in the magnificent work. This was the fruit of the labour of hundreds of men, of the bridling of human effort in a mathematical rationalization, of a force of will which moulded stone and imbued it with a soul.

*"Under the custody of the Ah Kines, the
victim ascended to the temple. He held his
head erect and his muscles taunt, free of
fear. He was truely ascending to the gods..."*

It was a truely exciting experience to wander through the civic and ceremonial centre of the city. Keh was interested to notice that even those buildings which came together to form quadrangles in the same way as in Chichén Itzá were somehow different to those to which he was accustomed. The fact is that each city has its own spirit even when the peoples inhabiting them share the same customs and have reached the same level of technical attainment.

Keh later met up with his godfather in a previously agreed spot. He thanked the architect for his fascinating explantion and took his leave of him. Then, in the company of his godfather, they made their way to the house in which they were to be lodged. A large area had been set aside for the dwellings of the ordinary people since Uxmal had a large population.

Great was Keh's surprise on reaching Mayapan to find it surrounded by a protective wall. This gave it an air of mystery and ensured its power. At the gate, Ah Otz was interrogated by the guards on the nature of his mission since not all are permitted to pass through into the city. Satisfied that his reason for wishing to enter the city was authentic, the two were permitted to pass the gate. As they walked through the city, Keh was gradually overcome by a feeling of sadness. Ah Otz was aware of his emotions and chose to remain silent. It seemed that they had made a transition from a monumental world of marvels to another which was a mere hint of the other's greatness. The buildings were too small, they lacked grandeur. Here the temples did not rear up towards the realms of the divine, they merely served their function as places of worship. Mayapán however, which meant "banner of the Mayas" was a large city of considerable political importance since it was the seat of the confederation. It was founded in the year 941 and expanded under the rule of the *Cocom* family. They invited the *Tutulxiús* to construct their buildings. Keh could not remove from his mind the grandeur of the architecture of Uxmal or the beatuy of his own city and, therefore, could not understand why the architecture of Mayapán should be so unimpreassive in comparison. The sloping walls caused the boy to notice that the buildings showed the Toltec influence but its sublimeness was lacking. He stood for a while before a low pyramid which resembled a dancing platform and, although it was well hewn, he felt something bordering on pity. He was overcome with sadness and Ah Otz whispered in his ear: "Yes, it is true, our progress is drawing to its end, every thing is coming to a standstill, beauty is dimming, creativity is on the decline. It is Like a slow death, with long, intermittent pauses".

But Mayapán was fascinating in its own way, the whole city gave evidence of constant activity like boiling water. The population was large and seemed to generate life and human activity. Its inhabitants hurried and bustled, especially in the market place where the selling and bartering called to mind the flight and twittering of birds. Objets constantly changed hands and every face bore an expression of delirious delight in possession and acquisition. Here ownership was a constant and obvious desire. Equally apparent was the slave trade. Náhuatl men from Xicalango were hired to put down any move of insubordination or resistance. Many lords of the Mayab lived in this city, under the authority of the supreme *Cocom*. These lords governed their towns from Mayapán through the offices of subalterns. A smell of tyranny was in the air, very different from the atmosphere in Chichén Itzá. One could not, however, but be impressed by the size of the city. It was said that it was composed of over three thousand five hundred buildings standing on the banks of twenty springs.

Ah Otz decided that it would be fitting for Keh to accompany him when he went to bestow the grifts he had brought with him. There were no secret messages to be given since he bore only words of greeting and good will. Wearing suitably respectful expressions, they were taken before the Great Lord of the *Cocom* who was called Hunac Keel, a strict and powerful personage. He was surrounded by his retinue and all were attired in rich, beautifully worked robes. He accepted the gifts with expressions of gratitude, offered a dignified thanks and bid Ah Otz bear his best wishes to the Lord of the Itzaes, Chac Xib Chac, who was their leader at that time. Hunac Keel then offered Ah Otz a large collection of gifts to be given to his Lord. Everything indicated that peace reigned and that all was well with the Confederation.

Now that their mission had been completed, they directed their steps towards one of the gates in the wall. It was guarded by men of arms. However, they extended a friendly greeting to Ah Otz whom they knew to be of noble origins and who was, moreover, known to them from recent journies and recognized to be a worthy ambassador of the Itzáes. Once through the gate, they set off together on the return journey along the *sacbé,* the white road.

Ceremonies

It was the duty of children to become familiar with
the occupation of their fathers, in order to inspire greater respect and to equip them to understand their
fathers' destiny in life. From an early age, Keh became
aware of his father's position as assistant to the *Ah
Kines,* the Priests of the Sun, who consulted oracles,
presided over human sacrifices and the monthly ceremonies in honour of the gods. The *Ah Kines* collabo-
rated with the *chilames,* the prophets and interpreters
of the will of the gods who also acted as assistants to
Ahau Can, the Serpent Lord and high priest. Ah Tzab
performed many tasks in connection with the rituals
of the city He was in charge of seeing that the temples
were kept clean, that jugs of water were always at hand
and that the sacred fire never went out. He kept order
in the communal dwelling of the young women dedicated

to the priesthood which also housed those chosen for sacrifice. He checked that the *Ah caboob* paid the exact tribute corresponding to each district of the city and also held a post in the economic adminstration. He ensured that the groups of musicians were attended to and supervised the upkeep of the ceremonial robes.

Ken always held the priesthood in the highest respect, being aware that the traditions of his people were in their safekeeping and that they were responsible for ensuring that the greatest achievements of the Mayan cultural apogee were preserved. Years earlier, when the populus turned against the priests, the Mayan cultural heritage was greatly impaired. It was perhaps for this reason that, in Keh's time, the priests and the fighting men worked together. Although the influence exercised by the city and people of Tula had wrought some changes, the Mayan essence continued to flourish through the cult to their ancestors and a jealous guarding of tradition. From ancient times, the Mayans had practiced human sacrifice and Mexican influence had gradually caused the ritual custom to become more frequent in the Mayan regions. The *holcanes,* "the grave", "those of serpent's head", were responsible for obtaining slaves and sacrificial victims. Those of humble origins were used for hard labour. The men were called *p'entac* and the women *munach.* Only prisioners of war of high lineage were entitled to be sacrificed in holocausts to the major gods. It was considered an honour to die for the gods and serve as their staff of life. Many mothers voluntarily offered their children for sacrifice and others were born to this destiny. Others undertook great exploits in order to win the privilege.

Not long before, Keh had witnessed a sacrifice in

"A straw mat had been placed on the floor before
the assembled students that he might be seated,
but the old man preferred to walk to and fro as he
spoke. And thus he began to narrate the events
of the beginning..."

the temple of the Eagle and Tiger warriors. It had been prophesied that the peace in Chichén Itzá, which had lasted for 20 *baktunes,* would soon disintegrate into constant war. Hence, on this ocassion, hommage was paid to *Pakat, Sacal Puc* and *Ah Chhuy Kak,* the gods of violent death and sacrifice. The congregation was composed principally of young warriors whose boides were painted in red and black. The *nacom* or warrior chiefs displayed plumes of such bright colours that it seemed that they carried flames upon their heads while others wore plumes of black as an allusion to death.

A continuous chant followed the rythem of the *tunkules* which rang out through the fiery evening sky. It seemed that the flaming clouds might at any moment drop from the heavens. There was a feeling of great tension in the air, that of the combined wills of hundreds of individuals united in the same plea: "We ask for victory, oh gods, in the battles to come". The feet of the dancers thumped upon the stone platforms, they gestured, swung around and leapt in the air in mock battle. The victim was led up to the temple under the guidance of the *Ah kines.* He held his head erect, his muscles tight, free from fear. He was truly about to ascend to the gods. He was annointed and his masks and clothing removed that the gods might see his true features. The *pom* smoke enveloped his body. Four *chaques,* their bodies painted blue, laid the victim down on the sacrifical stone and took a firm hold of his arms and legs, his chest lay bear in offering and he turned his eyes heavenward. In spite of the distance which separated the spectators from the altar, they could still, even with their eyes closed, picture each step of the ritual: the cry of the *nacom* invoking the gods, his hand raised above his head grasping the flint, his assistants preparing the body and the lightening movement as the executioner buried the flint deep into the victim's chest plunging his hand into the wound and drawing out the heart of the noble-blooded victim and, finally, the clamour of the crowd at the sight of the heart held on high. The gods took their fill of the blood and the voices of the people chanting their petitions and wonder redoubled.

Soon afterwards, the corpse was thrown down the steps of the temple where other priests stood ready to remove the skin which was given to the *chilam* who wrapped himself in it and executed a solemn dance. Since the victim had been a brave and noble soldier, several ate of his flesh in order to establish a relationship with him. This strengthened them and allowed the spirit of the victim which had already been united with the gods to dwell within them.

Several of the sacrifices witnessed by Keh made a profound impression on him, allowing him to experience the paroxysm whereby a combination of joy and pain purify and lend sublimity to human transcendence. Keh would never forget the sacrifice in which the victim was killed by arrows. Tied to a post, a youth was prepared as a sacrifice to the gods. His naked, undecorated body showed his nobility and goodness. In a circle around him, the dancers began a dance, slow at first and gradually increasing in speed. They carried cross bows and arrows and an accompanying song indicated when they should release their arrows. They pierced the body at the long intervals required by the ritual. The blood flowed as from a spring, liquid red in the process of becoming divine, contrasted sharply with the blue painted skin. The prolonged agony was finally brought to an end at a sign upon which the archers aimed straight at the white mark painted on the breast of the victim to mark the postion of the heart. This was one of the first scenes painted by Keh in the codices, having witnessed it on several more occasions and duly studied its meaning in the books on the suject.

The next sacrifice witnessed by Keh took place in the Sacred Cenote. The preliminary rites took place in the great temple at which offerings were made to the gods with songs and dance. A crowd of over eight hundred waved paper flags in the air. *Ahau Can,* the high priest, intoned a series of prayers which were then repeated by the *Ah Kines*. It seemed that the dancers carried the mystery of the birds in their hearts, their plumes moved with the rhythm of the music as if it were their natural language and they were ignorant of the meaning of words, as though their sole means of expression was the song of the birds and the rustle of their feathers. Their steps required the utmost precision since they followed the passage of the stars and imitated their perfect balance. The preliminary ceremonies at an end, the procession set out along the white path leading to the cenote. The priests headed the procession followed by several men, women and children who were to be the victims. The maidens were lovely to behold, the elder men filled with an air of dignity, the warriors virile and the children frollicked and played because they had been told that they were to leave this life to return to the realms of the gods. Behind these followed a group of warriors charged with the maintenance of order. The remainder of the citizens brought up the rear in straight, orderly lines until they reached

the very lip of the cenote. The sacrificial victims imme-
diatley entered the adjoining steam bath and were again
purified while the people outside continued to sing and
dance, all filled with expectation.

The *Ah Kines* reappeared with their retinue of sacrificial victims. The *nacom* awaited them on the platform.
The people flung *pom* and jade into the sacred waters
and finally, the victims were thrown in after them. They
plunged into the depths were they would look upon
Chaac, the god with features of jade. The ceremony
seemed to have come to an end when suddenly one of
the maidens reappeared on the surface. The gods had
chosen to spare her life, she had been snatched from the
jaws of death and returned to life as a worthy messenger.
A clamour arose in the crowd. Ah Tzab and others
rushed forward to fling creepers down to the girl and,
when she finally caught hold of them, they hoisted her
up onto dry land. She was borne to the priest's dwelling
on a stretcher of entwined reeds and silk cotton tree
branches. The crowd waited silently outside to be informed of the nature of the divine message. Despite the
passing of many hours and the anxiety of all those
of calm. Finally, *Ahau Can* appeared on the threshold
and announced the contents of the message sent by
Chaac: "Our jade has become part of the face of the
Lord of the Rain who has communicated to us through
the maiden his satisfaction and pleasure. We have
brought the gods great contentment. They are pleased
with our offerings and promise to protects us with
their power". A light, gentle rain began to fall on the
upturned faces of the onlookers. Cries of joy rose from
the earth to the heavens and the people expressed their
graditude through dance and song. The merry making

lasted for several hours; soaked to the skin, the crowd gave voice to its feelings of good will and joy until slowly the gathering disbanded, each returning to the shelter of their homes.

Life in Chichén Itzá centred on ceremony. Ritual served to give form to thought, to establish concepts and maintain the cosmic order. Excitment had been high throughout the day but, exhausted as they were, the young men of the city discussed the events that they had just witnessed and told of other ceremonies that they had witnessed. Hence, talk turned to the new year ceremonies, held during the *Uayeb* month which was that of the five days of misfortune. Hommage was paid to those who ushered, in the new year, carrying upon their shouldres time and events. The bearers were the *Kan* years associated with the east, the *Muluc* years with the north, the *Ik* years with the west and the *Cauac* years with the south. Preparations were made to reverence the *Bacaboob,* patrons and augurs of the years which they represented as well as the *Uayeyaboob.* During the days of misfortune, people were likely to go mad, to become dark or to lose their features since, though brief, this was a period in which chaos reigned. These days were associated with death because it was the time in which death was in decline. Evil influences lay in wait. For this reason, the people remained in their houses, hidden from the evil forces at large. Thus hidden, they devoted their energies to sweeping the floors, painting the walls, sharpening their knives and destroying all the old household goods. During the closing hours of the *Uayeb* all the people gathered with the high priests and *chaques* in the city's rubbish dump, to burn and bury the remains of these items. Thus, the people took their leave of the year just ending which had been devoured by death and awaited a new awakening. This was the time for repainting the buildings, restoring the murals and laying the foundations of new constructions. The skills of the craftsmen in both textiles and ceramics were stretched to the full during this period.

A different celebration was held during each of the months of the year. The new beginning was celebrated during the first month of the year which was called *Pop*. After fasting through out the days of the *Uayeb* and accomplishing the necessary penace, the people were in readiness to carry our exorcisms and cast out abominable spirits which was a necessary preparation for any festival since it produced clarity of thought. New *chaques* were elected and it was their task to light the new fire and burn *pom* in the braziers dedicated to each and every one of the gods after which they drank *balché* until they reached a state of total inebriation. This feast was in honour of all the gods, great and small, and was presided over by the jaguar deity.

During the second month, *Uo,* whose patron was the god of the number 7, the priests, *Ah Kines, Chilam Balames* and other augurs dedicated their celebration to *Kinich Ahau Itzamná.* This restival was referred to as *Pocám.* The great books were purified by a substance disolved in so-called virgin water which was water drawn from places to which women had not had access. There followed an account of events which were to take place during the year in question and other necessary predictions were issued. The ceremony closed with a dance called *Okot uil.*

During the *Zip* month whose patron was the Serpent,

the ceremonies were dedicated to three different ends. The doctors and healers paid hommage to *Ixchel, Itzamná, Cit Bolon Tun* and *Ahau Chameh,* the gods of medecine. Simultaneaously, the hunters made offerings to *Acanum* and *Zuhuyzipitabai* who were the gods who protected those in this occupation. The ceremonial dances recreated events of the hunt and imitated animals. For their part, the fishermen sought the favour of *Ah Kak Nexoy, Ahpuá* and *Ahcit Dzamalacum* who held fate of fishermen in their hands. The dance they executed on this occasion was called *Chohom* and the dancers were decorated with shells and the sound of conches filled the air as at no other time during the year. Numerous human sacrifices were made during that month, providing sustenance for both god and man.

The bat was the patron of the *Tzot* month during which time no festivities were held since it was a period of preparation, fasting and purification, especially for the beekeepers since their ceremonies were held the following month.

Cabán, the god of the day was the patron of the *Tzec* month. This was the time for honouring the *Bacaboob* and especially *Hobnilcabab* of the *Kan* years. All festivities during this month were bloodless in order to ensure an abundance of honey.

The celebrations of the month of *Xul* were dedicated to Kukulcán. In every city boasting a temple in his honour, processions bearing bright, symbolic plumes went to pay him homage. On the evening of the 16th day, after fasting and complyng with the prescribed penaces, the ceremony of the reconsecration of the idols began. This event was called *Chic Caban* and lasted five days and nights, during which time nobody was permitted to leave

"The victor who supervised the military actions of his triumph and the capture of the vanquished by his warriors..."

the temple except the actors who went from place to place enacting the mythical drama of Kukulcán. Food was taken without salt or chili.

Yaxkin was another month of preparation. Its patron was the sun and, hence, the period was associated with the clarification of ideas. Several days were set aside as being particulary propitious for meditation.

The Old God was the patron of the month *Mol* and celebrations were held in honour of all the gods. Children received a great deal of attention and participated in many of the rites perfomed during this time. They were thus initiated in their future duties to ensure that they were proficient by the time they reached adulthood and would learn to love the tasks they performed. The beekeepers were responsible for the beautiful aspect of the festivities since it was their task to adorn the place with flowers in abundance so that the gods would nurture their bees. Numerous wooden idols were carved during this month. In order to imbue these idols with an awareness of the vast numbers of gods they represented, many were re the human sacrifices offered to attract the presence of the gods. This feast was called *Olob zab kam yax*.

The month of *Chen* whose patron was the moon, was dedicated to beggars. The idols carved during the preceding month were sanctified and took their places in those spots chosen for their worship. The owners of the idols rewarded the craftsmen who created them with gifts of birds, animals and cacao.

The planet Venus was patron of the *Yax* month. The ceremony on this occasion was called *oc ná* and was dedicated to the *chaques* or gods of the corn fields. The temple was also renovated on this occasion. The clay idols and their incense burners were changed and stones commemorating the event were erected.

The patron of the *Zac* month was the god of the *uinal* or period of twenty days. Feasts were held in honour of *Acanum* and *Uuhuyzipitabai* to placate their anger over the blood shed and the animals killed during the hunting expeditions. Vows were taken to never kill an animal simply for the sake of it but only when the need for food justified the death. The hunters expressed their sorrow for having had to kill and performed dances imitating animals and sang in their honour.

No festivities whatsoever were held during the *Keh* month whose patron was the New Fire. It was a month related to the passing of time, cycles which began and ended and the abundance of days and years.

A Young God was the patron of the *Mac* month. The celebrations held were in honorur of the *Chaques* and of *Itzamná,* that they might bestow rain on the maize. The ceremony was completely dedicated to agriculture and the old participated in the ceremony, symbolizing the land· that had been exhausted through cultivation. The *Tupp Kak* rite took place two days before the main ceremony and was connected with the *Tzolkin,* the sacred calendar.

Daily hommage was rendered to the gods during the *Kankin* month but no other festivities took place. A Young God also presided over the month of *Muan* which was the time when the cacao plantation owners honoured the gods *Ek Chuah, Chac* and *Hobnil.* The following month, called *Pax* was the time of the *Pacum Chac* when the leaders and priests from all over the area gathered in their principle cities to keep vigil for five nights in the temple of the god *Cit Chac Coh* that he might bestow on them victory in war. The *nacom* or warrior chief was borne through the city with great pop and ceremony and the martial dance called *Holkan Okot* was performed before him. The *Kayab* and *Cumkú* months were those during which the *Sabakil Than* festivities were held in the houses of the leading dignitaries.

Recalling to mind all these ceremonies, the youths could not but recognize the sumptuousness of these occasions. Although they had many features in common, one had but to look at the ceremonial robes to identify who presided over the events to know which ceremony was in progress. The rites and dances performed also differed according to the occasion. Music was, of course, one of the principale elements of these feasts. The musicians playing the *tunkules* were highly skilled in their art. This was a drum made from a hollow trunk, generally of the marmalade tree, with an opening in the part that served as a seat and two hollows at the upper end, each producing a different tone when struck with a ball of rubber. Some were beautifully and intricately worked and their resonance was such that they could be heard at great distances. The *zacatán* was a similar instrument. It was a large, cylindrical drum, also fashioned from a hollow truck with a single opening covered with hide. Turtle shells struck with deer horns served as percussion instruments. There were wind instruments such as long, slender trumpets; flutes of cane, wood, bone and clay; sea conches; ocarinas and whistles. There were further instruments such as timbrels and reatles. The music was pentapharic and could be played with a trueness of tone and precision that fully met the requirements of the rituals.

The beginning

A deep, inner pleasure dwelt in the hearts of the Itzáe people. The whole town already buzzed with news of the arrival of Sactenel, an elderly and wise quiché from the highlands. He was held in such high esteem that the name they had given him, Sactenel, was that of a god and meant "He of the White Flute". He had a prodigious memory, he knew all that had ever happened, since the beginning. His memory recorded time and events, later to recount them. He was history personified. He visited Chichén Itzá every seven years to impart his knowledge that it might not sink into the depths of forgetfullness and ignorance.

As soon as the *tunkules* and conches sounded, the people throughout the city clamoured: "The great Sactenel has arrived, he who knows who were the first men, our ancestors; he who has knowledge of the mysteries of past generations and the sequence of the kingdoms". It was to Sactenel and other wise men like him that the people owed their knowledge of cities founded in former, splendourous ages; the cities which were no longer inhabited, which had fallen into ruin and had been overrun by weeds and those which were still visited during the great ceremonies.

The young men living in the communal dwelling had fasted for seven days in absolute silence, thereby purifying themselves in readiness to listen to the words of the wise man. It was not easy to absord details of the passing of time but the young men were eager to learn. Sactenel did not usually employ the language of Yucatán but spoke in the tongue of the quichés which was very different and therefore they would have to pay close attention to catch every one of his words that they might repeat them and never forget. The young men would repeat to their children all they heard that day and their children would pass them on to their own offspring. Knowledge would hence pass from generation to generation. This is ample proof of the power of the word through time. In this way tradition was never broken or lost. It became eternal.

On his arrival, Sactenel was first greeted by the great men of the city, the *kines, chilames,* those who hold the sun, wisdom and greatness. They went out to meet him in the great hall and bowed before him and listened to his words. Sactenel had spent his whole life traveling from city to city and so it was that he brought news from other parts. He had but to speak with the person who occupied the highest position and held the sceptre of power to be able to foretell the future in store for the city. He was wise and therefore the leaders paid heed to his counsel. But, on this occasion, he was in

"The city is protected from invasion
by a great wall on three sides and is
flancked on the fourth by a wall of natural
rock bathed by the sea..."

Chichén Itzá, and was engaged in conversation with *Halach uinic*. He informed the lord that the peace which has reigned for so many years could well be destroyed if due harmony was not maintained within the Mayapán-Chichén Itzá-Uxmal Confederation. Already the *chilames* and augurs who gazed upon the sacred waters of the cenotes spoke of possible wars. Sactenel was familiar with the past, right from the very beginning and the future was not closed to him. He even spoke of white, bearded men who would come from across the great waters and would become lords of those lands and of the people. He thus prepared them, so that events would not take them by surprise and to open their hearts to accept the happenings borne by the Lords of Time which would be deposited in future years.

The first light of day crept over the horizon and hardly had the light begun to spread across the earth and give shape and form to things when the young men were all prepared and waiting to enter the presence of Sactenel. The old man shortly entered the hall and all bowed their heads and laughed softly to show that this was an occasion of great joy for them. The youths were alert and eager. A rush mat had been placed in readiness before the group of listeners for the old man to sit upon but he preferred to pace to and fro as he spoke. And then he began to speak of the beginning and these were his words:

"The beginning was silence. Only the sky existed and there was no life. Such was the peace that reigned that it seemed not to exist. Then there was the sea, which was calm in the company of the immensity of the sky. The face of the earth was nowhere to be seen. Man, bird nor fish existed. There were no crabs, trees, stones, caves, hills, grass or woods. These marvels had not yet been wrought. There was only immobility and silence in the darkness of deepest night. Only the Creator, the Former, *Tepeu, Gucumatz,* the Progenitors resided in the waters in an aura of light. They were hidden beneath feathers of green and blue and for this reason they were called Gucumatz. They were beings of great wisdom and deep thought. And this was how the sky existed and also the Heart of the Sky and this is the name of God".

When he had spoken thus, the old man made a long pause. He walked between the young men and read the astonishment on their faces and felt their eager thirst for knowledge. All remained completely silent, they barely breathed and all eyes followed the movements of their teacher. He again began to speak, this time in the Mayan tongue of the city of Chichén Itzá. He omitted no detail, recounting events word by word, gesture by gesture. And he then reverted to the quiché language, repeating his exact words and gestures. Then he summoned the youngest of the group, instructing him to repeat word for word all that the master had spoken. And the youth gave a fairly accurate rendering of the events recounted, with only a few hesitations and omissions. Then he called forward another boy, instructing him to be seated on the rush mat and give his rendering. Another was instructed to correct his companion's version. Next, several boys narrated it together and then all voices became as one and their memories were thoroughly stetched. Finally, the old man picked up from where he had left off and continued:

"And then the word was born and in the darkness, in the night, *Tepeu* and *Gucumatz* spoke together. And each sought the opinion of the other and they meditated and they came to an agreement and united their words and thought. And this was the beginning of harmony and of this harmony, of this agreement, life arose.

"And it became obvious to them as they meditated that as soon as it became light, man should appear. Then they prepared the creation and growth of trees and reeds and the birth of life and the creation of man. It was thus arranged in the shadows of the night by the Heart of the Sky who is called Huricán".

"The Heart of the Sky has three components. The first is called *Caculhá-Huricán,* the second *Chipi-Cal-culhá* and the third *Raxa-Caculhá.* These three together form the Heart of the Sky".

He fell silent, the time had come for a much needed pause. Again he walked among the young men. He gazed into the very depths of their beings. He gauged their understanding at a glance, nuturing them with his eyes. He then repeated his narration in the Mayan tongue of Chichén Itzá and proceeded to question them, first individually and then in groups and finally all together. He gave a final rendering to impress it for ever of their minds and then continued:

"Then *Tepeau* and *Gucumatz* held cousel together on life and light, how to bring about the dawn and who would produce food and sustenance.

"Let this be done! Let the empitness be filled! Let the water draw back and leave dry land, let the land arise and take its place! These were their words. Let it be light, let the day dawn in the sky and throw light on the earth! Our creation will be devoid of glory and grandeur until the human creature, man, is formed. Thus they spoke.

"Then they created the earth. This is the true tale of how the earth was created. Earth! they said, and it came into being.

"Until then, creation had been as mist, as cloud, as dust but when they spoke, the mountains reared up from the sea and rose up".

"Mountains and valleys were formed by magic, it was a prodigy and immediately cypress goves and pine forests, appeared on their surface.

"And Gucumantz was filled with gladness, saying:

"Wonderous has been your coming, Heart of the Sky: you *Huracán* and you, *Chipi-Caculhá, Raxa-Caculhá!*

"Our work, our creation will be finished", they answered.

Sactenel again fell silent, and invited the young men to repeat his words, this being the nature of the mnemotechny, the art of improving the memory. It seemed that his narrative had been engraved indelibly upon their minds. Their lips repeated his words without hesitation or uncertainty, such was their interest, their amazement, their desire to absorb knowledge. Sactenel continued, saying:

"This was how the earth was created, when it was moulded by the Heart of the Sky, the Heart of the Earth which is the name given to those who first brought life to its surface when the sky was suspended and the earth was as yet covered in water. And their work was gradually brought to perfection as they brought their creations into being after much reflection and discussion".

The time had come for the midday meal and all over the city the people sat at table except in the comunal dwelling of the young men who animatedly continued their studies. They felt no overwhelming desire to eat as they had had much experience of fasting. Their interest lay in continuing their learning. They were as vessels receiving a continuous flow of water. The words of Sactenel fell as sweet rain upon their ears, clarifying their spirits, or as seeds which fertilized their minds. He continued as before, with continuous repetitions, to relate how the creating gods formed the first animals, birds, reptiles, fish and mammals. The nature of each was different, some ran and leapt across the land or dragged themselves along the ground as reptiles, the fish thrived in the depths of the ocean and yet other creatures flew in the air. But these creatures, though beautiful in their vitality, did not have the gift of the word, they could merely croak, howl, cackle or whistle. They did not have the capacity of thought or the means to venerate the gods, their creators. And hence the deities knew that they had not yet created the perfect being with the ability to pay hommage to them, to speak and invoke their names. And so they decided to create a being which would seek its food and make its home in the valleys and woodlands. And it was destined that they should eat each others flesh as nourishment. Their flesh would be sacrificed and their fate was that they should die on the face of the earth.

And so the gods, needful of adoration and homage and of the presence of some being on earth which would be aware of their existence and would sustain them, they moulded the flesh of man from clay. And the young men heard and repeated the following words:

"But they saw that their work was not good because it became brittle or remained soft, it had no movement or strength, it fell and was not rigid, the head did not move, the face slid to one side, its sight was blind. It spoke from the beginning but had no understanding. It became damp in the wet and dissolved".

In this way, the boys became aware of the first divine attempt to create man and they learned that it had been unsuccessful and that the gods enlisted the aid of *Ixpiyacoc, Ixmucané, Hunahpú-Utiú*. . . And so the "Forebearers of the dawn and of light" held conference with the augurs and prophets and meditated. And the young men repeated the following tale:

"Give us your opinion, *Hunahpú-Vuc, Hunahpú-Utiu*, twice mother, twice father, *Nim-Ac, Nimá Tziís*, Lord of the emerald, the jeweller, Lord of the green gourd, master of resin, grandfather of the sun, grandfather of the dawn for thus will you be addressed by our work, by the creatures of our making. Read your grains of maize and the *tzité*. And the old woman called *Chicracán Ixmucané* and the old men of the *tzité* called *Ixpiyacoc*, consulted the maize and said that it would be well to carve the eyes and mouth of man in wood. And so it was.

The thoughts of the young scholars travelled back down through the centuries and their minds dwelt with the gods of the beginning. They pictured the gods carving wood, fashioning man from a branch. The wood of a type called Pito was used for the male dolls and the females were fashioned from reed mace. And their understanding which became ever clearer saw how these creations peopled the face of the earth. They had the gift of speech but had neither soul nor reason. They multiplied and had sons and daughters but they wandered without purpose on all fours. Their faces were haggard, their hands and feet limp. They had no blood, no vital juices or solidity. Their flesh was yellow. And the young men recited:

"They did not meditate nor speak with their Creator, their Former, he who had made them, who had created them. And for this reason they were left to die and wiped from the face of the earth. *Xecotcovach* came down and dug out their eyes; *Camalotz* cut off their heads; *Cotzbalam* descended and devoured their flesh. And *Tucumbalam* also came and crushed their bones and nerves and ground them to dust and scattered it".

Upon hearing of the destruction of the second divine attempt to create man, the youths were filled with mirth to hear how the grinding stones and the animals turned against man. seeking vegeance for their sufferings at the hands of man, torturing their tormentors and repaying them for all the evil they had done to the animals. The grinding stones ground them, the heating dishes burnt them and the animals beat them and destroyed their faces and their bodies.

Hours had passed in these teachings about the beginning, night had fallen on the earth. The young men were tired but eager to learn more. Nevertheless, Sactenel proposed that they should continue their labours the following day. A murmur of disappointment rose in the hall, the boys were longing to hear about the successful culmination of the god's labours in the definitive creation of man. Sactenel smiled and suggested that they should at least relax for a while and stretch their legs. And the boys walked to and fro, backwards and forwards, discussing and commenting on what they had heard. They were struck by the pride of *Vacub-Caquix,* he who had created the sun and the moon who, out of vanity, when the faces of the sun and the moon and

"Mucuy had learned to prepare maize in different ways: as pancakes (uah), as a drink (za), as a stew (keyem), and as flour (kah)..."

the stars were not in the sky, had sent the flood as a punishument to kill the wooden dolls whose lack of understanding made them blind. As they conversed, Sactenel spoke in a much lighter vein although his words were no less interesting, of how the young deities *Hunahpú* and *Ixbalanqué* resolved to put an end to *Vucub-Caquix* who vainly believed himself to be the sun, and to his sons *Zipacná,* who claimed to have created the mountains and the earth, and *Cabracán* who maintained that he was the mover of the earth and the heavens. And so it came to pass that as they quarreled over their greatness while they ate, they were done to death with blow guns. And so the sun and the moon were avenged for such vanity and, after many exploits, there was at last true brightness because one became the true sun and the other the true moon and the four hundred luminous youths who were killed by *Zipacná* also ascended to accompany them, in the form of stars. The old men told them of all these deeds and they took his teachings to heart and were astounded at the hardships encountered at the beginning. They were still engaged in discussion when several attendants entered the hall to bring them food. Each one received one and a half maize pancakes and a bowl of chocolate drink. They ate slowly because to hurry was to abuse and show little consideration for the goodness of nourishment. When they finished eating, all meditated and prepared to continue their learning.

Sactenel told how *Yac* (the mountain cat), *Utiú* (teh coyote), *Quel* (the parrot and *Hoc* (the crow) brought the gods news of the existence of the white and strength and health and it went to create the strength yellow ears of maize which grew in *Paxil* and *Cayalá*.

They led the gods to these lands of plenty. And there they found nourishment and food in plenty and this went to form the flesh of man, of this he was created, of this his blood was formed. *Ixmucané* ground the white and yellow ears and made a new drink which brought strength and health and is went to create the strength and muscles of man. The flesh of their forefathers, the four men who were created, was composed entirely of maize.

The youths enthusiatically repeated:

"The first man was *Balam-Quitzé,* the second *Balam-Acab,* the third *Mahucutah* and the fourth *Igui-Balam.* These are the names of our first mothers and fathers".

"When they had been created", continued Sactenel, "the Creators sent them to look upon the world. And they spoke and understood each other's words and they walked upright and marvelled at creation. Their intelligence was such that they could embrace all that existed, both divine and terrestial. Their wisdom was as great as that of the gods because they had understanding of the whole universe. For this reason the gods again gathered together and spoke as follows:

"What should we do with them now? Let the scope of their sight be reduced that they contemplate but a small part of the face of the earth! Their words are not good. Surely they are merely simple creatures of our making? Or are they to be gods as well?" Fear was struck into hearts of the deities when they saw that men were like to them in so many ways and it was decided that the nature of man should be changed. The Heart of the Sky created a mist before their eyes and they became clouded like the trace of breath on a mirror. Their eyes were dimmed and could see only what was near them and the distance was lost in a haze. The wisdom and knowledge of the first four of human kind, the beginning and root of my race, was destroyed".

Consternation showed on every face. They were wounded deep within their beings to learn why man's sight was so short and his understanding so little. Their hearts were filled with longing at the thought of those who, at least at the beginning, could see and understand everything in the universe and in the divine realms. But Sactenel sought to give them heart at the sight of their saddened faces:

"We are not blind and there is more than enough for us to seek to understand! There are many lands to travel and many seas to cross and uncounted places to discover. Man's task is great and an abundance of gifts have been bestowed upon us. Not only do we live upon the earth but we also build on it. If this seems small fortune to you, let me tell you that there is still a lot to see and a great deal to be achieved. If the gods have deprived us of the divine attribute of absolute intelligence, they have nonetheless endowed us with human properties and their potential has still not been fully explored".

When he finished speaking, Sactenel left the room with a bearing that showed both humility and an absolute conviction of the truth of what he had spoken. He went unhurriedly and his step displayed his absolute gratitude to his gods and creators.

In search of Chichén Itzá

Keh attentively examined the murals (Upper Temple of the Jaguars) which depicted interesting scenes of battles waged by the Itzáé people. These were indeed the antecedents of the foundation of Chichén Itzá. The narrative sequence showed the lords who shared a common, Chontal inheritance and, since they were fighting men at heart and also merchants, they competed against each other, first for the rich booty of Petén and later for Chakanputun and the subsequent control of the area.

The protagonist and his rival were represented over and over again in every scene and their importance was emphasized by the fact that they were larger than the other figures which was a sign of their elevated position in the hierarchy. Futhermore, their headdresses and emblems served to identify them. The emblem of the protagonist was the Plumed Serpent while that of the rival was a Solar Disk which also bore a Chaac mask. Some of the figures were painted in positions alluding to a manual of the martial arts and the military exploits were so clearly identifiable that Keh was able to reconstruct in his mind all the events that occurred during the different periods. There were scenes of ambush, combat, human sacrifice and the fate of a plundered town.

Keh's attention was caught by a scene in which the rival warrior chief bowed in submission before the victor who was supervising the military operations called for in time of triumph such as the imprisonment of the troops of his vanquished foe. Numerous were the naked, bound warriors being led to the sacrificial altar. The sequence relating the conquest and exile were full of drama. It showed women, for whom all hope had died, bearing their possessions on their backs, as they were driven from their town. It was most important that the two warring chieftains be painted with the same grandeur, vigour and magnificence of attire and there was a final gesture of reconciliation which showed that, although the rival had been conquered, recognition was nevertheless given to his great intelligence.

The background landscapes were also of great interest and, when he looked at them closely, Keh recognized the mountainous terrain of the low and rugged red hills (possibly in the south of Oaxaca or in Tabasco), the central lowlands (the Petén of Guatemala) and the calciferous stretches of his native land (the Yucatán Península).

The murals were proof of a masterly draughtsmanship and a control of colour and simultaneously fulfilled two

"*Keh had worked for a year under the supervision of the astronomers and high priests on a codex containing a chronological table and precious glyphs showing sixty nine dates...*"

functions, one decorative for its beauty and the other didactic for its content. Mayán art was subjective, mystical and highly symbolic. It was executed in accordance with aesthetic precepts particular to that culture and the artist's range of expression was strictly limited to a series of variations into which the inherent symbols of knowledge had to be integrated. A god had to be painted with all his attributes and attendant symbols to ensure that the figure was immediately recognized. Hence, most symbols served, in fact, as means of identification.

Seated on the floor before the murals, Keh painted several figures in certain positions and meticulously set down all their symbolic signs, the emblems of persons and cities, in order to familiarize himself with all the details contained in this historical narrative. As he drew with a flowing, sure hand on the amate paper on the floor before him, he incorporated further symbols which he considered to be related to the murals. This was not idle recreation, he was shortly to take an examination to demostrate his narrative ability in the field of codex painting. He rapidly retraced the history of Chichén Itzá in his mind and commited to paper a pictorial narration of the arrival of a group of Itzáes in the region of Siyan Can Bakhalal (today Bacalar, Quintana Roo) at the time of *Katún* 8 *Ahau* (159-179). On the following Katún 6 Ahau (179-199) they discovered Chichén Itzá (Mouth of the Well of the Itzáes) which was the name given to the cenotes. and they settled in the place after leaving Bakhalal where they resided for a period of 60 *tunes*. They settled in Chichén Itzá on *Katún* 13 *Ahau* (238-258) and remained there for ten score *tunes* (approximately 200 years) when they emigrated to Chakanputun.

That ocurred on *Katún 6 Ahau* (435-455) and here they dwelt for thirteen score *tunes* after which they returned to Chichén Itzá on *Katún 8 Ahau* (672-692). Later, the Itzáe people wandered homeless for two score *tunes, Katunes 6 Ahau* and *4 Ahau* (692-731) and it was not until *Katún 4 Ahau* (711-731) that they returned to Chichén Itzá.

The rendering of dates was no mean achievement but Keh had had enough practise in this art to be able to put them down without error, ensuring that they were immediately identifiable to avoid confusion.

He painted the introductory glyph twice as large as those that followed it to make it stand out while in the central part this could vary considerably since there were nineteen different forms according to the patron god of the month in which the calculation of the number of days occupied by the tale fell. The chronological units of the Long calculation were represented in the Initial Series from left to right and from top to botton in either one or two columns. The *Baktunes* always came first. Numerals were represented by the dot and dash or by their equivalent in "heads" and "complete bodies". The various chronological periods were represented by their own individual hieroglyphics or in the above-mentioned form. It was not difficult to recognize the numeral corresponding to the day to which the name was related. The total number of days had only to be divided by thirteen. When it was exactly divisible, the corresponding numeral was the same as that of the date 4 *Ahau* (zero). If it was not divisible, the number remaining was added to 4 (of 4 *Ahau*) leaving a total of thirteen or less which was the numeral corresponding to the name. If the figure remaining was more than thirteen, thirteen was subtracted in order to arrive at the correct numeral. The position of the day of the *Tzolkin* in the month was arrived at by dividing the total number of days by 365. Keh made a rapid practice calculation, picking a date at random: 1.416,600 divided by 365 gave a quotient of 3881 with 35 left over; he advanced 35 positions along the *haad* calendar from 9 *Cumhú* to find the corresponding position which fell on 18 *Pop*. Since there were seventeen positions between 9 *Cumkú* and O *Pop* of the following year, he subtracted 17 from the number left over (35-17), leaving him with the number he sought (18) which obviously fell during the first month, *Pop* (*Pop* 18).

The Long Calculation had been commonly used during the time when the city was in ascendance although it was no longer current. Nevertheless, Keh had been obliged to learn it in order to be able to recognize the inscriptions on the older buildings. He was also familiar with a more straight forward system (dating from the end of a period). This method indicated a certain period of time transpired and the date on which it ended. Hence, only three hierogliphics were required to express it: the number of a *Katún* or *Tun,* the hieroglyphic of the corresponding day of the *Tzolkin* and the corresponding position of the month. An example might be the final date of the *Katún* 16 period — 2 *Ahau* — 13 *Tzec,* which corresponded to the Initial Series 9.16.0.0.0 2 *Ahau* — 13 *Tzec*. The most commonly used inscription in Chichén Itzá was that arrived at simply by consulting the Calendar Wheel. Many appeared on the lintles of the buildings such as 8 *Manik* 15 *Uo* — (Lintle 2 of

Las Monjas) and 9 *Lamat* II *Yax* (Temples of the Four Lintles in Chichén Itzá). The dates of the Calendar Wheel repeated themselves every 52 years of 365 days each year. Another simplified method of recording dates, used by the *Chilambalames* (Medium Calculation) was that whereby a date was repeated every 265.25 tropical years. When it was said that Chichén Itzá was discovered on *Katún* 8 *Ahau,* 8 *Ahau* meant that the event ocurred in a *Katún* or period of 20 years of 360 days (7200 days) and that it ended on the day 8 *Ahau*. The thirteen numerals which gave the name to each *Katún* of the series and which preceded the word *Ahau were* fixed in accordance with a rigourous and inalterable order: 13, 11, 9, 7, 5, 3, 1, 12, 10, 8, 6, 4, and 2. The explanation behind this sequence was that the number of days of the *katún* (7200), had to be divided by 13 giving a quotient of 554 with 11 left over. This figure, added to whatever the number of the day on which the *Katun* ended, gives another number which is that of the *Ahau* falling at the end of the following *Katún* after subtracting 13 from the above total if it was over 13.

Since Keh had long studied and practised these systems they seemed to him quite straight forward but no less fascinating for that. This urge to record time was one way of fighting against death. Time flowed as water through the hands, thought Keh, but by intelligence it could be set down with the aid of mathematics and so be engraved on stone for eternity. Things of the past are recorded and we can gaze upon the face of time.

While Keh was thus engaged in exercises of calculation and recording, he was interrupted by Ah Tzab who entered in great haste with a shadow of grave preoccupation upon his features.

"The birth of the baby is overdue, the midwife says that it should have been born by now. The gods of death are obstructing its path, they refuse to allow it to reside on the earth, they refuse to allow it to experience light and nature and song. Your mother is seriously ill and we must go at once to the island of *Ixchel,* to beg her to spare the infants life and clear its path".

Keh was much concerned about the health of his mother and saddened to learn that his brother's or sister's advent in life had been frustrated; he gathered up his work materials and left the temple to accompany his father on the pilgrimage which was to be made in the hope that *Ixchel* would see fit to bestow her favours upon them.

Journey to Cozumel and Tulúm

The canoe in which they travelled was tiny in comparison to those used by the warriors which required between thirty and forty oarsmen. Ah Otz and Ah Tzab rowed while Cuzam lay on the bottom of the boat with her head resting in Keh's lap. The pain which she tried to hide caused beads of sweat to stand out on her forehead and, when it grew too great, she struggled to suppress muffled groans. The canoe slid easily over the surface of the water, the calmness of which seemed to pressage death. They made their way between the dual blues of sea and sky. In spite of the anxiety caused by his mother's pain, Keh could not but feel a deep pleasure in the immensity of the ocean which he had for so many years longed to see. The sea was a manifestation of *Chaac's* companion, the one robed in water, she who is eternally reproduced and who grows in infinity.

Cuzam had finally fallen into a doze and the oars

shattered the reflection of the moon which had already risen high in the sky and dappled the disturbed water with her light. The stars danced on the waves as though the gods were bathing, purifying themselves and reviving their spirits. A pyramid was visible in the distance, seeming to arise uncannily from the waters. "It is Tulum", explained Ah Otz, "it used to be called Zama, the city of the dawn". In times past, when *Halach Uinic* died, his body was taken for burial to the island of Jaina, a sacred place. The funeral procession started out from Tulum. *Ah Kines* took the lead, burning incense along their path over the waters and intoning prayers and chants. The corpse was borne by his successor and the great high priest, the chilames and the warriors followed on behind them. All were richly attired. Their iridescent plumes changed colour in the bright light. The funeral cortege was indeed a magnificent sight to behold".

A groan escaped Cuzam's lips and she twisted and turned in her pain. The men threw all their might into their rowing. It was a race against death, a fight for life and the canoe seemed to be surrounded by infinitely long stretches of water on all sides. But an opposing current, like hopelessness itself, hindered their passage. Keh turned his eyes to the moon in mute supplication, willing her to heed his plea. And there was goodness in the gods who aided men; the canoe smoothly crossed the opposing current and sped upon its way. The warm, humid air appeased their fears.

No sooner had the canoe come to rest on the sands of the island than a group of men and women came to their assistance. Cuzam was borne upshore on a stretcher of reeds. A priest and four healers awaited her in the temple of Ixchel. Keh and Ah Tzab presented

"Nevertheless, a friend gave Cuzam a small
white dog that her dead husband would
be sure to have a companion. Ah Otz, who had
finished digging the grave..."

their offerings of *pom* and jade and then proceeded to pierce their ear lobes and tongues in self sacrifice. As their blood flowed warm, the godess Ixchel gave proof of her bounty. A feeling of peace descended on the suffering woman as the gods of the underworld ceased to threaten her. A cry rang out through the still air and Cuzam gave birth to a girl. Life had triumphed over death but Cuzam had been much weakened by the strain and loss of blood and would have to remain in Cozumel for some days to regain sufficient strength to undertake the return journey. The women had taken her to the steam bath and, as water was poured over the glowing hot stones, the small, underground cavern filled with steam. Her body was rubbed with medicinal herbs and massaged. The circultation of her blood quickened and the evil presence was removed from her body as the sweat ran from her pores. The prayers of the healing women drew the forces of good to her.

Ah Tzab remained in Cozumel with his convalescent wife, while Ah Otz and Keh decided to take advantage of the forced delay to visit Tulum. The canoe gradually drew closer to the city across the water. In the light of day, the pyramid which they had glimpsed rising from the water the night before, was even more astonishing. This beautiful castle which absorbed the clean waters and light breezes of the sea truely existed and was no a mere appartition in the shadows of the night.

The city was protected from invasion by a high wall which surrounded it on three sides while protection on the fourth side was afford by a natural rampart of rock washed by the sea. Tulum could be reached by either land or sea and many were the travellers who journeyed to it.

Several steles stood in the main square, recording important dates. One of these, adorned with a warrior chief bedecked with a great headdress, bore the date 8 *Ahau* 13 *Ceh* (433AD) and no doubt alluded to the founding of the city. Another bore the date 564BC and the remainder recorded the dates of different successions to the throne.

There were no more than fifty buildings, many of which showed evidence of superimposed additions in different styles of architecture. The population of the city was small since it was inhabited only by important personages who held political and religious sway over the fate of the surrounding cities.

As they walked through the streets of the city, they saw a group of slaves, who were immediately intentifiable by their short hair and by the fact that they were clad in only an *ek* and went barefoot, bearing large bundles of food. Shortly before the arrival of Keh and Ah Otz, several canoes bearing merchants and their goods, led by the *ploms* as the most wealthy merchants were called, had brought supplies to the beaches of Tulum before continuing on their way to other nearby cities.

Keh was particularly struck by a small temple, painted blue, which was dedicated to the Descending God, Venus, who was submerged in the underworld for eight days every year. Close at hand there stood a building painted in red and black in which the *nacom* or warrior chieftain dwelt. Other temples and buildings stood round about, all of different shapes and sizes but blending together in perfect ahrmony.

It was the *Pax* month and the day came to celebrate the feast of *Pacum Chac* which was dedicated to *Cit Chac Coh, Pakat, Sacal Puc* and *Ah Chhuy Kak,* the gods of war. The *holpop,* "he who is seated on the rush mat" was borne in solemn, festive procession to the temple in which the sacred instruments were kept. These were distributed to the musicians who immediately struck up a harmony full of cries and messages. Thus, the sound could be heard of the *kayab* and *bexelac* of turtle shell; *chul,* flute; *hom,* trumpet (of clay, wood or fashioned from a gourd); *cayum,* clay timbrel and, above their combined snoud, could be heard the thud of the *tunkul* and the *pax* which were made of hollow trucks with jaguar skin stretched over the opening. The instruments were played by the *Ah paxboob.*

The *nacom,* also seated on a rush mat, was carried to the main temple with a retinue of 200 warriors. As soon as he had ascended the last step of the flight leading up to the temple, the warriors began the martial dance called the *holkan okot.* It was a reconstruction of battle and the warriors brandished their swords, wooden clubs (*hadžab*), slings (*yutún*), darts and lances. They bore shields for protection as well as padded tunics. The air was alive with excitment created by the beat of the instruments and the shouts of the dancing warriors.

The dance continued for many long hours as the warriors changed rhythm and simulated ambush and combat. In the main temple, masked priests clad in the attire of the war gods held religious council. The festival came to an end when the priest presiding over the sacrifice held aloft the hearts of the victims.

From Tulum, Ah Otz and Keh proceeded to the bay of Zamabac, in the Mayan province of Chetumal where the best canoes of the time were built and where an abundance of honey was produced. Ah Otz exchanged a large supply of honey for *ha* which was the Mayan word for cocao seeds. Thence, they travelled on to Ekab whose inhabitants owned rich salt flats. The land was marshy thereabout and the sea flooded the land at high tide. The people then dammed up the mouth through which the sea water had entered to prevent it from escaping and, as the water evaporated in the sun, a thick crust of salt was eventually produced. This was gathered and ground to a fine white powder. Ah Otz purchased several sackfulls and, after taking his leave of Keh, he headed south where he would exchange the salt for jade, idols and other objects and food.

Keh returned to Tulum to find his mother fully recovered from her ordeal and eager to return home. The baby girl was very small but the priest had assured her that the child would grow strong and healthy and would have a long life. A final ceremony of gratitude was to take place before they left. On this occasion, the umbilical cord and the placenta had not been buried under the hearth as was the custom. Instead, they had been placed in a sea conch and were now flung far out to sea as a tribute to the gods of the sea and especially to *Ixchel*. When the rite had been performed, the priests and grateful family bowed to the four cardinal points from which both beneficial and harmful winds and natural forces arose. A sacred silk-cotton tree, provider of the first food of human kind, grew at each of these points: *Chac Imix Che* (the red tree of the east), *Zac Imix Che* (the white tree of the north), *Ek Imix Che* (the black tree of west) and *Kan Imix Che* (the yellow tree of the south). These coincided with the symbolic colours of *Bacaboob*, *Chaques* and *Pauahtunes*.

Mucuy's early years

As the priests had foretold, the girl child gained
strength and was of a sweet and gentle nature. It seemed
that she had been born with a natural joy in her heart.
She had been named Mucuy which meant "little turtle-
dove". And this was the name by which she was to be
known throughout her life as was the case with Keh
who, although he had received other names as he grew
older, was always called thus by his parents. The name
given to children immediately after their birth was known
as the *paal kaabá* (which was the equivalent of a baptis-
mal name). These were often the names of animals,
plants or objects. Later in life the prefix *Ah* was added
to boys names as seen in the names Ah Otz and Ah
Keh. In the case of girls, *Ix* or simply *X* was added:
Ix Cuzam, Ix Mucuy. Later, the paternal surname was
added: Ah Keh Kumun, Ix Mucuy Kumun. A further

*"There is something more important
that you should see, a magnificent tomb, for
great was the lord who lies there..."*

name, known as the *naal kaabá* was given during the *emkú* ceremony (the descent of god), in this case the word Na (mother) and the maternal surname were interjected in front of the paternal surname: Na Chi (Cuzam's surname) Kumul. *Coco kabá* was the word for nickname and alluded to a particular personal characteristic for example, Mucuy was often called "she who is always laughing".

When Mucuy was taken for the first time to the priests to enquire into her destiny, she was given objects related to household tasks. However, in the ceremony of the "descent of god", she was given objects related specifically to spinning since *Ixchel,* her protectress, was the godess who invented this art.

As was the custom for both boys and girls, she was left free during the first years to play and watch her mother in her household tasks and she even went so far as to try and copy all Cuzam did. And she reached an age when she was well versed in all that had to be done about the home. She loved to go to the market and knew very well what had to be bought. She was aware that only the strictly necessary should be purchased. "Never waste life", her mother warned her, "for if you do, the gods will deprive you of what you most need".

Mucuy had learned the art of preparing maize in several different ways, as pancakes (*uah*), in liquid form for drinking (*za*), in a stew called pozole (*keyem*), as pinole flour (*kah*), and tamale (*muxubbak*). At the break of day, as she prepared to make the pancakes for the day, she drank a cup of maize drink with the rest of the family. She loved the smell of maize as she toasted it ready for grinding. Sometimes cocao was added to the drink. During the course of the day they ate a little pozole stew. She also knew how to prepare the large lumps of maize dough which could be kept for a long time without loosing their flavour or nutritional value. At dusk they ate a more hearty meal of pancakes, chili and cooked black beans called kabaxbuul. She had also learned the recipe for a dish made with ground pumpkin seeds. And, since the meals had to be varied, she sometimes cooked fish or meat dishes or vegetable stew.

The girl had also learned to spin and sang as she worked in the belief that it would please Ixchel who would improve the results of her labour. She knew the secrets of dying thread, especially wool. At home, she had sown several dye producing plants and others were available in the market. There were two particular plants which were essential for this work, the *Yinch-kaan* (jacobinia) and the *Chi Té* (eugenia). Wool was brought to the boil with a few handfuls of eugenia thrown in and, when it had simmered for two hours, it was allowed to cool and then washed. The jacobinia was not boiled but simply left in water until it fermented. Both were colour fixatives. The *Tzon té* (moss) did not grow in the nearby hills but merchants brought it to the city from other areas. This was used to produce dark brown tones. *Kan ak* produced yellow and *Cha té* black, *pitz otz* blue, *makob* purple or mauve according to the amount used and *chil te uet,* which were small fruits called "monkey droppings", produced shades of green. There were also dyes from other sources such as *batzi chuj* or the cochineal insect which were tiny parasites to be found on cacti.

Mucuy was careful to keep her cooking and dying utensils apart since many of the plants used for dying were poisonous. Whenever she dyed cloth she washed the vessels out with great care to ensure that no colour remained to spoil future dying. Cumuy loved colour, she enjoyed dying and her favourite cloth was the soft cotton produced in the city.

Keh took it upon himself to instruct her in other matters such as teaching her to count from one to twenty, as a tiny child she had already memorized them: *hun* (1), *ca* (2), *ox* (3), *can* (4), *ho* (5), *uac* (6), *uuc* (7), *uaxac* (8), *bolon* (9), *lahun* (10), *buluc* (11), *lahca* (12), *oxlahun* (13), *canlahun* (14), *holahun* (15), *uaclahun* (16), *uuclahun* (17), *uaxaclahun* (18), *bolonlahun* (19), *hunkal* (20).

The numbers one to four were represented graphically with dots, five was a horizontal dash six to nineteen were a combination of dots and dashes. There were also hieroglyphics corresponding to each of these numbers in the shape of human heads and sometimes human bodies. The skull was the representation for the number ten or, more precisely, the lower jaw corresponded to the value of ten. When this bone was taken in combination with the heads representing the numbers three to ten, the number was automatically increased by ten. Hence, the head standing for the number nine combined with the jaw bone represented nineteen. The numbers eleven and twelve each had a particular hieroglyphic.

The Mayan system of counting was vigesimal and the value of a number was determined by the position in which it was drawn. Any position could be occupied by the sign for "totality" which was zero or any of the numbers between one and nineteen. In this system, twenty units of any order consituted one unit of the order immediately above and, hence, the constant factors corresponding to each position, from the bottom upwards are successively: 1; 20; 400 (20 × 20); 8000 (20 × 20 × 20) and so on.

Keh had learned all this as a young child and, when he was older, he had also been taught that certain modifications were introduced, according to the periods used by the astronomers. The number 360 was used as the factor in the third position in the place of 400 which actually corresponded to this position. This was done in order to use the multiple of 20 closest to 365, which was 360, to form a *tun* which was used as a chronological unit. The Mayan astronomers were well aware that the tropical year was a little over 365 days but, since they did not have fractions in their numerical system, they took the year to be 365 days and the system was indeed viable, provided that time was exactly recorded and periodic adjustments made.

The *Kin* and *Baktun* periods were commonly used in the "long calculation" and spans of millions of years could be calculated on the basic of this system:

Kin: one day
Uinal: 20 *kines* or days
Tun: 360 *kines* or days
Katun: 20 *tunes* or 7,200 *kines* or days
Baktun: 20 *katunes* or 1,444,000 days
Pictun: 20 *baktunes* or 2,880,000 days
Calabtun: 20 *pictunes* or 57,600,000 days
Kinchiltun: 20 *calabtunes* or 1,152,000,000 days
Alautun: 20 *kinchiltunes* or 23,040,000,000 days.

This was all very difficult for Mucuy to grasp since she was still very small, but Keh patiently explained it to her over and over again that she might understand the passing of time and its order. Time held a fascination for the Mayas, both young and old. Hence, mathematics constituted an integral part of the philosophical thought behind chronology.

Although the rest was somewhat out of her reach, Mucuy had, nevertheless, fully grasped the meaning of the *Kin,* the unit of time corresponding to a day. She watched the sun from its rising to its setting and had even deliberately remained awake for a whole night to experience the passing of the dark hours. She knew that the dawn was called *yahalcab* or *zazhálcab;* the early hours *hatcab kin;* midday *chumuc kin* or *chunkin;* the evening *okinal* and the sunset *emelkin* or *ochkin.* The night was called *akab;* twilight *kaz akab,* midnight *chumuc akab* and the moment before dawn *potakab.* She learned that it was the sun *Kin* who generated time and that its movement breathed life into time, its presence was light, its absence darkness. While the sun lived, so would man.

The códices

Keh would have liked to dedicate his life exclusively to painting codices but, the human heart, like the sun, is in continual motion caused by emotion. The ideas of starting a family held its attractions for him. To him it appeared a means of transcending his own existence, imbuing his offspring with a warmth of spirit and a love of life itself. For this reason he had decided to marry Ix Canul but *Ixchel* had not looked favourably upon her, something sterile in her womb prevented her from conceiving. But they hoped with prayers, pilgrimages, offerings and the tending of an undying flame on the hearth to one day receive the bounty of the godess. Nevertheless, the life shared by the couple was sweet and full of hope.

Keh went daily to the House of the Codices where he worked with great meticulousness and care. Here he painted and studied glyphs. The world of the glyphs was indeed extensive and it seemed to him that a single life time would not be sufficient to learn all there was to know about them. There were new glyphs because the world was ever-changing and writing evolves.

Great volumes of work had already been completed. They were in accordance with the prophecies of the *chilames*. The *kunes* were not only units of time of 7,200 days in length but also periods heavy with events to be narrated. Life was considered to be like a wheel which turns and returns. Events might be periodically repeated in the katunes of the same name and this gave rise to the katun-based prophecies which foretold what would occur in the following katun.

The sun sank its teeth into the moon or the moon into the sun, the tiger into the moon, the serpent into the sun; this was the image representing the eclipse. The correct sequence of possible eclypses could be established on the basis of the sacred calendar of 260 days. Keh had been working for a year, under the supervision of astronomers and chilames, on a codex featuring a chronological table and precise glyphs containing the dates of sixty nine solar eclipses in a period of thirty three years after which the table could be used again from the beginning in accordance with the law of repetition.

Another of his codices depicted the passage of comets and their appearance on earth. Their luminous trail brought sorrow to man. But their appearance could be forecasted. Hence, Keh painted the comets and in his codices showed past, present and future plagues and droughts.

He also painted everything related to the gods; their feast days and the human sacrifices which should be offered up to them. Whole illustrations were dedicated

*"Keh, remembering his emotion when he had
visited Uxmal, took his son to see it..."*

to the gods of agriculutre. Others depicted hunting and fishing expeditions. Some showed the tributes offered to his people, the number of inhabitants of the city, the state of its economy, the trade links which stretched ever further afield to distant cities of other cultures. The world was expanding! Beyond the range of their sight were other lands, other palaces and even other gods. And Keh set down all that was told to him for posterity.

And so he spent his days, dedicated to his work, loving to his wife until Ix Canul finally announced the glad tidings that they were to have a child. This was reason enough for a celebration. Cuzam, Mucuy and other women busied themselves with the preparations. On this great occasion, *balché,* the sacred drink, was to be taken in the paternal household.

The elders had taught Keh that everything repeated itself and Keh now saw for himself that this was true. He had seen Mucuy in her cradle, the birth of his own children, the journies to Cozumel, daily work, the omnipresence of the gods, the annual ceremonies. Merchants travelled, astronomers discovered stars, architects constructed buildings. And, as life went on, so the population of the Mayan cities grew and the towns increased in beauty. *Kin,* the sun, shone down every day: life continued its course.

New generations of children had to be educated, new faces would abide in the communal dwelling of the young men, new generations of farmers, fishermen, scientists and wise men and rulers would take their places in the world. And the Tzolkin calendar would be consulted over and over again to learn the destiny of every new being.

But all in the world was not life, death also took its share. The gods *Bolontikú* of the *Metnal* demanded sustenance.

The presence of death

The month of *Yax* drew to an end and so too the *Oc ná* celebrations. The ritual of the breaking of the idols had gone on day after day to make way for others in the temples, idols of fresh clay, newly made in a general renovation of the divine images. The stucco work of the great buildings had been freshly painted, the bright colours contrasting sharply. Ah Tzab had been kept very busy supervising and organising all these tasks. He had selected new robes and instruments to be placed in the chamber were all the sacred attire and utensils were kept. Ah Tzab himself now wore a new *ix* and sandals and a light, as of inner rebirth, shone in his eyes.

As Cuzam served supper to her husband, she listened attentively as he described all the details of the ceremonies that he had been organizing over the last few days. Each year was the same, with the same changes succeeding each other. She was pleased but, at the same time, experienced a feeling of anxiety like a knot in the stomach. With strange premonition , she became aware that Ah Tzab was about to undergo a great change. "Perhaps a change in attitude to life", she thought, "or a natural progression with the increase of age". Her mind dwelt on all things that change, feeling satisfaction and fulfillment.

A grimace of pain appeared on Ah Tzab's face. The tensing of his muscles and concentration of his strength gave him an expression as that of an infant in the moment of birth: on a threshold, but this time that of death. With the speed and brightness of a comet, the events of his life flashed before his eyes. His life was to him as a falling star shedding light and banishing shadow. It was the great moment of discernment.

Ah Tzab bent double and tumbled to the floor. Cuzam's screams and weeping prevented her from going immediately to his aid. Her efforts were in vain and she rushed to the door and her frantic shouts brought the neighbours running. It was not for nothing that man lived and developed in a community that he might be equipped to face and resolve problems, not for nothing did he learn to dominate the hopelessness he feels in the sight of suffering. Society was the common spirit jointly bearing the designs of the gods and the manifestations of nature. And, for this reason, the neighbours did not hesitate.

They all gathered around Ah Tzab, the friend who was no longer with them. An old woman lifted his limp wrist and announced that the minor pulse, that of the body, had ceased while the major pulse, that of the soul, had escaped to the realms of *Bolontikú*. All knelt, bowed their foreheads to the ground and intoned a prayer to help the dead man to leave the earth without nostalgia for it, that he might enter untiammeled into the underworld, the destination of all who left the flesh, who have been freed from material burdens.

"Your time has come to die", said the old woman, "your time to leave the earth, to rid yourself of all to which you had become accustomed, your home and your dear ones. You must leave the earth, deprive yourself of its beauty and its sadness. Do not glance back at what you leave behind, that your spirit might have the strength to overcome the obstacles that you will meet on your journey after death. You will wander far and spend four years in the deep passages of the *Metnal,* you must seek out the gods and, in their company, you will stand in the presence of mystery".

A few of the company departed to go and inform the priests, others remained to help the bereaved wife. The women swept the floor, the men began to dig the grave. With Mucuy's help, Cuzam bathed the body of Ah Tzab, ritually anointing his feet, perfuming his body and dressing him. Keh rushed into the house to see if it was indeed true that his father had died. He approached the corpse slowly and thoughtfully: "Many are the men who come to people the earth, and the same number leave it. None remain here. The earth, body and time are but on loan. Father, now you will have to retrace every step of your life".

Chaques wearing masks representing bats, owls, red serpents and black serpents and other animals symbolizing death presided over the ceremony. Ah Tzab was prepared for burial and the priests filled his mouth with *keyem,* ground maize, that he might have sustenance on his journey. In the case of rich men and of the Great Lord, a piece of jade, which was considered as money, would be substituted for the maize. In this way, the dead man could use the jade to purchase favours from the gods and persuade them to reduce his time of wandering in the *Metnal*. But Ah Tzab was of the people, a servant of the priests. But he was, nevertheless, provided with maize to eat on the way.

The great lords, rulers and priests were buried in the company of five servants to ensure that they received protection and aid on their journey. It was an honour for servants to be buried with their masters because this guaranteed the protection of the Great Lords of the Night. It earned them divine admiration and their loyalty and services would not go unrewarded. The greatest of men were cremated, if not the whole body, at least a part of it, and the ashes conserved in clay jars which were in fact delicate urns over which temples were sometimes built. Alternatively, the ashes might be placed in the hollow neck of a wooden statue. The opening to the cavity would then be closed with the scalp of the dead man and the rest of the body buried.

It was traditional to bury corpses with a dog, especially a tame one which had been a friend of its master in life, that the animal might bear his master on his back over the broad river of raging water which had to be crossed on the way. Hence, it was important to win the affection of dogs, treating them with kindness and anticipated gratitude. Ah Tzab's dog had died many years before and, before burying him, his master had asked him to wait for him on the bank of the river. Nonetheless, a friend of the family gave Cuzam a small, white dog to bury with her husband to ensure that he had company

"Muan was examined by the Kaat
Naat, the questioner. "You have a reflective
mind", said his teacher, "an intellectual
mind. You are eager to learn"...

on the journey. When the grave had been dug, Ah Otz placed the animal at the dead man's feet. Friends who had come to bid their last farewell brought gifts that would be useful along the way: jars of food, tortillas, water, necklaces, sandals and finely carved stones were placed in the grave beside the body that Ah Tzab might offer them to the gods as gifts. Then the earth covered him.

It was the custom of the people of that city to bury the dead in their own homes. In some cases, the family preferred to leave the house altogether but others lived quite peacefully in the knowledge that their forefathers were buried under the floor. It had been decided that Cuzam would go and live with Keh but she would nevertheless pay a daily visit to the house in which her husband had been buried. She would go to sing to him and tell him of all that was happening in the city, to take him food and water in case he should need them. This would continue for at least four years.

As soon as the ceremony was over, joyful music encouraged all present to return to their homes and carry on living. Ah Otz approached Keh and whispered in his ear: "There is no better moment for you to make your own judgement as to where to direct your sentiments and, moreover, to form an opinion with respect to the passing of time".

Not without sorrow, Keh smiled and answered: "Everything can be divided and changed, we are one thing and then another. Let us hope that my father is happy with the change that has come over him and that the gods will look favourably on him".

Journey to Otulúm

Since his father's passing, Keh's mind was preoccupied with thoughts of death. He frequently questioned the sense of existence and meditated on burial and funeral rites which varied in accordance with the social and economic standing of the deceased. This obsession led him to visit Otulúm (Palenque), "fortified house".

Keh and Ah Otz had had to make a long journey through the jungle, where the heat stifled them and the song of birds mesmerized them, to reach the religious centre. They followed the path along the banks of the Otulúm River and noticed, when they reached their destination, how the builders had channeled the river into an aqueduct, part of which was open to the sky while the remainder was covered by a dome. They were much impressed by the sewage and drainage system which was connected to the steam baths and adjoining lavatories.

There were numerous temples in the place but the very dimensions of the main building, the Palace, made it stand out from all the others. The symmetry of the stairway, which was flanked on either side by struts carved with figures in relief, invited the onlooker to ascend towards the realms of the gods. The building was composed of a series of galleries built around four inner courtyards. A great square-based tower, an astronomical observatory, rose from the centre of one of these courtyards.

The western courtyard was surrounded by four buildings, the walls of one of which was covered from top to bottom with hieroglyphics. A relief carving depicted four standing men in the company of several seated priests. Keh and Ah Otz passed down a stairway from the inner hall to one of the courtyards. Great figures carved in stone adorned the struts and inclines. Then they approached the foot of the tower and here Keh's eyes fell on a slab showing small figures of the Lords of the Night. The very sight of them incited the spirit to sing to the shadows and to death. What thoughts must have filled Keh's mind, wishing himself to people the infinite depths of these gods.

Ah Otz drew his attention to a temple situated to the west of the Palace, saying: "There is something more important that you should see, a tomb which is magnificent because great is the lord who lies within it". They made their way to a building consisting of nine staggered sections, symbolizing the various levels of the *Metnal*. The facade of the temple was directed towards the north, the cardinal point of their forefathers, the gods of creation. When they reached the top they came to the entrance of the temple which had four square columns and five doors. Each pillar bore a stucco figure surrounded by divine symbols to watch over the entrance. The walls were of turquoise blue on a red background, seeming to recreate the chromatism of sun and sky. The feet of each of the stucco figures stood on a hideous, haggard face of the deity of the Earth. In their arms they bore a child with a serpent's head. Keh exclaimed: "This must be the representation of the birth of the four *chaaques,* the assistants of the god Chaac."

They entered the temple and Ah Otz showed Keh the spot in the sanctuary floor where the tunnel leading down to the mortuary sanctuary opened, penetrating the very heart of the pyramid. Although the tunnel contained a stairway, it was strictly forbidden to descend to the crypt but Ah Otz had with him a book which showed all that it contained. "Look, this is what is kept inside", he explained to Keh, "here the great lord is protected by six young nobles and by the *Bolontikú* themselves. The gods are modelled in stucco, six are standing and three are seated. Their headdresses are indeed magnificent, each representing a different bird connected with death. They are richly attired and each holds in his hand a serpent-handled staff. Look, here you can see masks of the rain god".

Keh reflected a while and murmured: "I can picture the gods of death picking to pieces flesh, memories, nerves, shadow and weeping. What then remains of man's earthly roots? What other strange existence lies in wait for him in exchange for his flesh and dreams? What is the nature of non-being? What winds dissipate his longing for earth?

Ah Otz smiled and slapped Keh on the back and directed his thoughts along another track: "Death is only a joining of man and time, a return to his origin and then repose in a ancestral sea of ashes, particles of light and shade which acquire life in the immensity of the universe. And the fact that the dead are close to the gods does not mean that they forget the living, their offspring. You yourself are well aware of the presence of our forebearers on earth".

"Is the great lord stripped of flesh? But he must be protected in some way?" asked Keh. Ah Otz showed him the book: "He lies protected in the very heart of this building specially constructed to lodge him in greatness. In the centre of the crypt is a huge sarcophagous, the sides of which are carved with the history of the priest and ruler. Ten figures are depicted, six men and four women. Each bears a plant on his back and some are wearing headdresses of birds and one of a jaguar. They arise from the earth, the place of their birth and their bodies move ever foward until they find paradise".

"In which direction does the body lie?" "The head is directed towards the north, the threshold or our ancestors. He is richly attired and magnificent are his robes. Upon his brow lies a diadem of jade from which hangs a disk of the Bat god, the muse of the underworld related to fertility on earth. A large jade bead was placed in his mouth which was a symbol of his heart, to be surrendered to the gods. His hair is parted into locks and adorned with jade. The intricate rings in his ears are magnificent. A string of beads of different shapes hangs about his neck. He was adorned with many beads, 200 went to make each of his bracelets and his breastplate is composed of nine strings of twenty one pieces each. A statuette of the solar deity was placed at his feet and his body is entirely surrounded by finely carved pieces of jade".

"What pains me most", murmured Keh, "is that the face disintegrates". "Not in the case of this great lord", eternalized, he was given a mask of jade which exactly reproduces his countenance".

Ah Otz again drew Keh's attention to a page of his book: "The body is covered with a great slab (8 metres square) which is engraved both on top and on all four sides. It shows the hideous mask to the muse of the earth and of death with open jaws devouring the body of a great man who is descending into its entrails in which one of the paradises is situated. Other images are also depicted such as a grain of maize, a conch cut lengthwise and an ear of young maize". "Of course", interrupted Keh, "they are the symbols of the birth of this divine planet and of the birth of man because our flesh was formed from maize. But, tell me, who is this great lord?".

"His calendar name is 8 Ahau. He was a great priest and ruler. The gods united with him and for this reason he became a deity; he has the attributes of the Sun, Venus and Chaac. A cross-shaped maize plant grows from his body. See how it stretches its shoots towards the sky. It is the tree of life which sprouts in the west of the belly of the godess of the earth. That is why he is crowned with the symbols of the quetzal bird and the mask of Chaac. These imply sacrifice and penitence, at the moment when the Earth devours Kin, the Sun, which is again thrown into the task of creating another day".

"Now", said Keh, "I feel all his greatness, teaching and eternal presence". "Yes", agreed Ah Otz, "a psychic bond links the sargophagous to the sanctuary at the top of the pyramid. From here, the priests can communicate with him and so learn his bidding and communicate it to the people. It is a pity that we are but common folk and do not deserve such a privilege. But tomorrow priests will arrive from cities all over the land to enter into contact with him".

"*The spears were raised to heaven to then
be driven deep into the hearts of men.
The death knell had sounded for the warriors
of Chichén Itzá...*"

The birth of Muan

At times life and death overlap as though they are a single happening. Flowers and fruit grow from decomposing matter in the earth and sometimes, from a dying body, life may arise like a hope in its continuation, a testimony to transcendence.

It happened that, next to the *chultún,* the drinking water cistern, Ix Canul, Keh's wife, was found dead. There at the water's edge, alone and without assitance, she had given birth to her child, a son who had forced his way into life several months before his time. She had not long been dead when they found her and it was apparent that, in spite of the quantity of blood that she had lost, she had been able to attend to the new born child, severing the umbilical cord and covering him with her ragged shawl. Cradled at his mother's breast, the infant awaited his first contact with the rest of the human race. News travels fast in any town and all heard of the event with astonishment and perplexity. Cuzam, the grandmother, in the manner of the most ancient mother of the gods, took upon herself the care of the child.

He was given the name Ah Muan which was one of the symbolic birds of the underworld. It did not occur to anybody to cast on him the blame for his mother's death for she had thus been permitted to go forth to meet the gods. Death in childbirth had made her a *Cihuateteo* according to the precepts of the Toltec religion and so they knew that her final resting place was in the paradise called *Cihuatlapan,* "place of women". There she would serve *Kin,* the Sun. Warriors who had fallen in battle, those who lived in the west, went to receive Kin with dancing when she rose from the underworld and accompanied her, all the while performing mock battles, along the curved route of her ascent. At the zennith, the *Cihuateteo* awaited her and it was they who accompanied her during her descent. And so a procession of female deities followed the sun as she sank, accompanying her to the very threshold of the underworld. This occured day after day, the solar retinue performing its task with absolute precision. It was said that every fifty two years, the warriors descended to earth in the form of humming birds and other precious birds to fill the hearts of women on earth with love and wonder. The *Cihuateteos,* however, appeared with haggard faces in search for their children for which they yearned. Fear was struck into the hearts of the children that saw them, all the more so because these women had the power to turn them into mice. Therefore, during the season in which these women were wont to appear, children's faces were covered with agave fibre masks to discourage the women from approaching. But it was only during this period that they were feared since, during the rest of the year, they were held in honour and esteem as companions of the sun.

When the oracles were consulted on the suject of the destiny of the child as dictated by the gods, the priest said: "This infant has been highly honoured. He will be an augur, Great Chilam among the Chilam Balames. Prodigious is his tongue, his voice will be heeded by all. He shall be called Muan because he will announce bad tidings for the future. He is messenger of the *Bolontikú*".

And the relevant instruments were buried under the hearth; precious feathers, the staff of death, a fish bone which was the symbol of sacrifice and the red and black soil of wisdom, the oracle.

Muan's intelligence was truely astounding. He was first among the children of his age to learn to walk and talk. He could calculate time with amazing speed and soon reached an age where he spoke as though he was in possession of great knowledge. The gods told him what to say, guiding his tongue and his lips.

Remembering the impression made on him by Uxmal, Keh took his son to visit the city. The child did not seem in the least surprised at the sights that were unfolded before his eyes and, standing before the great palace (the Ruler's Palace) he recited from memory:

"Beautiful is the city ruled over today by the Tutul Xius lords. The name is derived from the Náhuatl word Xiuhtótol, "turquoise bird". They are worthy sons of the Sun god and the Water god, of flame and of jade.

Beautiful creatures like in appearance to the chalchihuitl precious stones. They themseleves are the creators of beauty.

"They left their original lands and homes in Tulapan Chiconautlan (Tula) and went to settle in Nonoualcan, to the west of *Uuiná* in the *Katun* 3 *Ahau* (593-613). And there they settled for 4 *Katunes* and in the next one which was *Katún* 8 *Ahau* (672-692) they set out towards Chacnouitan which they reached after eigthy one years of pilgrimage. There leader was Chan Tepeau.

"They reached that land on the first *tun* of the *Katún* 13 *Ahau* (752) at the same time as Ah Mekat Tutul Xiuh. His people remained for 99 *tunes* (until 849) which was when the distric of Ziyaan-Caan was discovered in Bakhalal.

"During the *Katún* 2 *Ahau* (731-751) another Tutal Xiuh called Ah Cuytok settled in Uxmal. So, father, do not let them tell you that it was he who founded Uxmal because those who claim that this is so are merely seeking to unjustly glorify his name. The truth is that when Ah Cuytok arrived in this land that you now see before you, this city already existed, it had already been built by true blooded Mayan ancestors. This is the true history and it is borne out by the age of the stone and the features of *Puuc* architecture on top of which buildings of other styles have been raised. It is true that the Mayas of Uxmal were driven from their city and those who remained were vassals of the new masters.

Did you realize, father, that the Tutul Xiuh have reigned together with the Itzaés of Chichén and the Cocomes of Mayapán for a great length of time (200 years)? But we should mourn because this triple shared supremacy of the Confederation will come to an end in the *Katún 8 Ahau*. The League will be destroyed on the tenth *tun* (938) and we will leave Chichén Itzá".

Hardly were the sing-song, half-teasing words out of his mouth than Keh asked him: "Where did you learn all this? Who has taught you so much history, who revealed to you these events of the past and future?". Muan smiled and replied patiently: "I know. I have only to observe the Gods of the Temple and see what they carry. Some bring the "Great Fall", others war, others the building of new cities. It was thus that I learned of the arrival of the Tutul Xiuh. There are gods who have borne the Confederation of Uxmal-Chichén Itzá-Mayapán for almost 720 kines. But the League will come to an end in the *Katún 8 Ahau* (938).

"Destruction is nigh. We may feel its threat in the balls of our feet, it is spreading through our lands, it is reflected in the waters according to the gods of Time who are drawing ever nearer with their burdens of pain and change. Nothing can now be changed or prevented. This is what the gods bring us".

Keh grasped Muan's head between his hands, looked deep into his eyes and, more than admiration at his knowledge, he felt pain in the sight of this four-year old child whose destiny it was to have foreknowledge of ominous events. His father asked him "Does this make you suffer?" to which the child replied, "Yes, I suffer, but I seek comfort in the gods".

And so the child made his knowledge known to everyone and, for this reason, he was given the *coco kabá*, nickname, Ah Xochil Ich, "he of the owl's face" because his words, like the hooting of this creature, brought tidings of destruction and death. Muan was taken before the high priest and they spoke together for many

*"On 4 Ahau 8 Pax plague will
visit the land and wars will bring death.
Bearded strangers will be seen for
the first time..."*

hours. The young boy was already in possession of great knowledge and so it was decided that it would be harmful for the whole city to learn of his prophecies and it was consequently decided that he should go to live in the temple, in the company of the *Chilam Balames*.

The Suyuá Than

Muan recieved the privilege of being given a special
education. He was now put to study the *Suyuá Than*
"hierarchical, religious language", "the virgin word"
which expressed the enigmas of the cosmos, the dyna-
mics of time. This language was know only to princes,
rulers and priests. It was created by the *Chilam Balames* and was the tongue used for prophecies. Rarely
were the common people able to read between the lines
of these messages. This dissimultaion was required
because it was thought that false interpretations twisted
the mind and gave rise to strings of lies.

These so-called enigmas in fact gave shape and form
to philosophical thought and religious principles; a wide
range of knowledge and practises were derived from the
them in such diverse areas as ceremonies, military
operations, matters related to the calendar, politics, me-

dicine, science and techincal progress because it was considered that all man's activietes should be directed by laws which legitimized his being and his activities.

The images and terminology employed in the *Suyuá Than* were highly complex and appeared to refer to the supernatural although, contrary to appearances, it in fact dealt with simple, daily occurences which were down to earth and verifiable.

The chosen few had to provide responses to an endless number of enigmas, their abiltiy acting as a guage of their understanding of the mysteries and mental acrobatics required to express certain ideas in accordance with the necessary dissimulation inherent in sacred domains.

Muan was examined by the *Kaat Naat,* the questioner. "You have a thoughtful mind", his teacher told him, "a mind which is quick to understan. You strive after knowledge. But, tell me, what do you eat? Is it by any chance *keyem or kah?*".

Muan smiled: "It is jade (beauty) which nourishes me and also earth dissolved in water from the sacred cenote (the mysteries which can be understood by the chosen)". And then he added, "I feed on sound, I listen to everything; I feed on images, I look at everything".

"Where do questions originate?" asked the teacher.

"From astonishment", answered Muan "if one is surprised by something one is immediately inclined to ask questions".

"Good", said the *Kaan Naat,* "now bring me the sun, laid out on my plate, and sink the lance of the sky into its very heart. And the Great Tiger must be seated on top of it, drinking its blood".

Muan listened attentively to the command, thought for a moment and left the hall. A short while later he returned and placed the sun (a fried egg) on the *Kaat Naat's* plate, then he stuck the lance into its heart (blest it) and finally set the Great Tiger astride it (he poured chili sauce over it). This was the sacred egg used in rituals dedicated to the cult of the sun. Muan had correctly interpreted the words of the *Suyuá Than* and the questioner was much gratified.

"Tell me", said the questioner, "where in this hall are the jar and the underground water?".

"I am the jar", answered Muan, "I am the receptacle and you are the rain, the moisture of wisdom".

"What is the meaning of the moving flame which illuminates what lies ahead and burns everything in its path, leaving behind only ashes?" asked the teacher.

And Muan explained, "It means to reject without towards new clarifty of vision. As understanding reaches greater heights, errors of the past are shown in their true light. Whatever it costs me, I should cast aside any erroneous thoughts. One should rid oneself of any mistake. The moving flame is the desire for truth".

"Draw here the image of the god Tetrápode".

In response, Muan drew the image of Quetzalcoatl.

"I said the god Teptrápode, and he only has two feet".

"That is true", replied Muan, "but nevertheless I am correct, Quetzalcoatl, when he is given the name Nacxit ('four feet') Xuchitl ('flower'), refers to the fact that he posseses beauty (xuchitl) and is omnipresent (Nacxit) because he can travel simultaneously to the four corners of the universe".

"You have great knowledge", said the questioner, "you possess the universe".

"That is not so", retorted Muan, "because the finite cannot posses the infinite. I am mortal, one day I will cease to be. I merely summon up the truth which is perceived by my mind".

"What truth lies behind the words: they will kill the flower of Nacxit Xuchitl?".

"That man is destined to disappear", replied Muan, "that they will be divided by disputes and that beauty will die because there will be no priests or wise men to lead the people".

"The quest for truth, that is the task you set yourself", murmured the *Kaat Naat,* "and the way is lit by the gods for the one who seeks the truth. Go now and seek that light".

And so Muan's examination ended and he went back to his rooms. He had answered correctly and was capable of keeping to himself the secrets of the Suyuá Than.

End of the Mayapán league
The Itzáes are driven
from their city

The jade face of the god inhabiting the sacred well
of the water magicians had darkened. The mud had
been churned up, covering him and hiding him from
view. The waters changed from emerald green to black
then to the red of the blood shed in the quarrel.

Intrigues had been unleashed between Hunac Ceel
Cauich, leader of Mayapán, and Chac Xib Chac, lord
of Chichén Itzá. It was the *Katún 8 Ahau,* in the time
of the tenth *tun* (938), and the dispute was no longer
restricted merely to words. War had broken out. The
drums beat both night and day. Spears were branished
in the air, to then be thrust deep into the hearts of

men. Warriors of Chichén Itzá and those of Mayapán fell in battle. Death took its toll, the *Bolontikú* were satiated. Many were those who walked at that time in the *Metnal*.

"Who is this Hunac Cell Cauich?" asked *Kaat Naat*, "who today challenges and consumes us?".

"He is our enemy", replied Muan, "whose daring won him prestige and strength, he who flung himself into the depths of the sacred cenote of Chichén Itzá to learn its secrets and communicate the god's oracles to man. He sank and reemerged and, when he had climbed back onto the banks and pronounced the divine desire, he was declared leader, he who had merely been representative of a ruler called Ah Mex Cuec".

"And is it true that he descended to the very depths of the cenote?" asked the *Kaat Naat*.

"The *Suyúa Than* states that is was so", answered Muan. "In other words, he solved one of the enigmas. They sent him to bring back the yellow and white fruits. And because he knew the religious language and had knowledge of enigmas, he was made ruler".

At that time Hunac Ceel Cauich was a leader with great power, but he was of intriguing character. There was violence in his heart. And the wheels of prophecy instructed him to vanquish the Itzae people. The wasriors of Mayapán, under the command of seven chiefs with Náhuatl names, pursued the water magicians. The struggle was protracted and raged for 34 years. The Itzáes grew old as the blood flowed.

The Mayapán warriors set out to destroy Ulmil because its people had made a pact with Ulil, lord of Itzmal. Bonds of friendship and understanding were destroyed in battle and death. And the Itzáes were finally driven from their city. They were scattered under the raucous cry of the birds.

The sadness and grief of *Cuy* (the small black bird) and Icim (the owl) mingled with that of *Ix Dziban Yol Nicté* (flower of the painted heart).

Some refused to forsake their city and flung themselves into the wells to join their forefathers. Others had recourse to *Ix Tab,* the godess of hanging. Many were the silk cotton trees which bore a hanging human burden and all those who died at their own hand in this manner went to the paradise of *Ix Tab*. The exodus was sad. The Itzáes did not look back for fear of weeping at the last sight of the city which they had built. They had been despoiled of their former grandeur which now lay behind them. Children were carried on their parent's backs, the old leaned on the young for support and the long train of Itzáes followed their guides until they reached Taitza (Tayasal, a place in the Petén in the central Mayan region).

Life was recommenced in Tayazal. New buildings were erected and temples as dwellings for the gods. Vengeance was plotted in silence and none forgot their first city. The Itzáe people took solace only in memories of the past.

The great prophecies

Seated before a great vessel of virgin water, Muan meditated, prayed, sang and repeated the words spoken to him by the gods: the Itzáes would again engage the warriors of Mayapán in combat. The govenors of Hunac Ceel who had imposed his dominion throughout the peninsula by means of a centralist government were to receive their just desserts. Thoughout the duration of the Mayapán hegemony which lasted from 8 *Ahau* 8 Cumhú until 10 *Ahau* 3 *Mac,* the hate of the subject peoples was fanned by the arbitrary, oppressive methods and humiliation inflicted upon them. The hearts of the Mayas were to rebel and explode in a flower of blood, shields would arise, just as their hearts.

On 8 *Ahau* 3 *Mol* (1461) the destruction of Mayapán came about. The great cities were abandoned. The Mayas surged in every direction. Their cry was to be heard in the south and the north, in the east and in the west. Red was their cry and blue, white on every wind.

On 6 *Ahau* 3 *Zip* they were torn by the hurricane. On 4 *Ahau* 8 *Pax* they were visited by the plague and even then, war increased the death toll. The first bearded foreigners visited their shores (1511) and small pox, *Mayacimil*, "easy death" broke out among them. Mayas swollen of body with reddened skin, dry mouths and bulging eyes died by the hundreds.

No trace remained to tell the tale of the tyranny of the Cocomes and all was changed, despoiled and stricken with disease. Were the people to suffer Maní which meant "having finished" as coined by *Tutul Xiu,* leaders of the rebellion? Would the people suffer Tibulón, meaning "here we end" or "we have been taken as fools", coined by the last Cocom to survivie the slaughter. Nobody and nothing escaped, the cities and towns of Ah Canul, Ah Kin Chel, Canpech, Cochuah, Capul, Cuzamil, Potonchan, Chakan, Chactemal, Chikinchel, Ecab, Hocabá-Homún, Cehpech, Cehaché, Sotuta, Tases and Uayamil, not even the tiny villages, all places to which the settlers of the great cities fled were visited by hurricane, plague and battle.

By II *Ahau* 8 *Pop* (1559) everything had disintegrated. There were no priests to guide the people, there were no great leaders, only insignificant, uneducated masses. Decadence was painful. And the bearded men came and imposed their cross and their virgin and our gods hid themselves.

And Muan predicted: "Many *katunes* will the Mayas

live in slavery and only with the passing of time will
our ancestors arise in splendour and show their eternity.
Beauty will not be totally destroyed. The gods will again
show the light of their hidden faces.

When the waters of Quetzal, of the green bird Yaxum, draw back, when the children of women and the
children of men have been devoured, when great heaps
of skulls are piled up; after the great flood when the
mountains speak together on the curved face of the
earth above *Uuc Chapac,* seven centipede; after the time
when the fire burns in the centre of the flat land, when
fear must serve as nourishmen; when terror has been
inflicted by *Ah Uucted Cuy,* the Seven Owl, *Ah Uucte
Cahpat,* the Seven Centipede, when the people of the
earth, trees and stones, after the coming of *Ah Buluc
Ch'abtan,* the Eleven Faster, come to speak the word of
the Sun, the word arising from the hieroglyphic signalling
the wailing of the Itzáe people, the Water magicians;
when the Itzáes arise from the depths of their misery
and go out into the wooded, rocky lands to announce
their tidings of the justice of the Sun, the justice of the
Katún; after the possessor of the rush mat vomits what
he swallowed, what slid down his throat before he was
choked by the alms he received, when the sons of *Ah
Maax Cal,* the Prattling Monkey, have been betrayed;
when anger blazes from the countenance of *buluc Ch'abtan,* Eleven Faster, when he arises and extinguishes with
fire all that remains of the Itzáes in the third double of
the *katún;* after *Ichaansihó,* Face of the Birth of the
Sky, stoops to lift *Ah Itzam,* the Magician of Water
receives his heavy, painful burden, when the flagstone
shatters, the partridge whistles and the deer runs and

Ix Kan Itzman Tul, the Beautiful Witch of Gushing Water, is scattered in the plains, in the mountains under the eyes of the wise; after the time when infants and youths are multiplied and old men are fertile and old women conceive; when the end comes to the sway of *Buluc Am,* Eleven Carved Stone, when May Ceh the Deer's hoof, draws to a close and everything comes to an end and it is said: "The Itzáe people were here"; after *Ah Cantzincal,* the four corners becomes visible together with *Ah Can Ek,* the Four Darkness, *Ah Sac Dziu,* The White Thrush and *Ix Tol Och,* the corpulent Zarigüeya, assumes his place and there is a new word, a new teaching and pleas rise to *Ku Caan,* the Deity of the Sky and serpents link together, head to tail and new breeches are worn and new lords of the Rush Mat named; after the people have returned to the cave and well to take their fill of fear and beg the *Ah Kines,* Priests of the solar cult, when the precious cloak has been set in place and the belt of thirteen knots tied and the conutenance of the Ah Kin made square; when the gourds have grown large enough to make the cups and plates to accomoadate the water for which they beg, the left over crumbs of maize bread, the scant alms which they share between them: when *Ah Xixteel Ul,* the roaring earth conch, is angered and the evil *Xoox,* Shark, because they will be struck by fire and this is when the sharks will swallow each others tails and fire will strike the heavens and the clouds and the Itzáes will disappear, the Magicians of Water will disperse to the north and the west after they have crawled on all fours through their fields under the eagle gaze of *Ah Tzay Kanache,* the Sure Foothold, *Ak Kay Kin Bak,* he who Sells Meat by Day, *Ah Tooc,* The Burner,

Ah Dzuudz, The Haggard, and an end comes to the grinding of jade and precious stone and arrows rot in the presence of Kinich, Face of the Sun, together with *Buluc Ch'abtan,* Eleven Faster, who look upon them; after the jaguars have been deprived of their red and white spots, after the teeth and claws have been ripped from the jaguars of the Itzáes and great winds and mighty floods have come to pass and the countenance of *Ku,* deity of the Rush Mat and the Throne, is to be seen by all; when bones have whitened because these will be vicious years and *Ah Ox Kokol Tzk,* the Three collector of skulls, will fulfill his task, he is the sweeper of flat country which will be scorched with terrible sun and pursued with sudden death, days of thrist, days of hunger; after the passing of *Ah Cap Uach Tun,* He who orders the *tunes,* with his excessive misery and the thud is heard of the wooden instruments and the words ring out of *Ix Tan Yol Ha,* She who is in the heart of the water, and the corpulent Zaragüeya, *Ix Tol Och* laughs at himself for his changes in word and deed; after sudden death and disputes have been visited on *Ah Uucte Cuy,* the Seven Owl, *Chacmitan,* the Great Poverty, when the *katunes* clash when on the shore of the sea stands *Ah Maycuy,* the Deer Owl, in *Dzidzontun,* Place of Stones like Daggars and *Chac Hubil Ahau,* very Rebellious Lord, is present in *Sinhomal,* Place of Soap Plants and the time comes to pass when the entrails of *Kukulcan* the Plumed Serpent, are scattered and *Ah Chichic Soot,* he who plays the tamborine, draws back; when the *katún* leaves the cup overflowing with misery and great is the hunger inflicted by *Ah Uaxac Yol Kauil,* the Eleven Sacred Heart, when the *katún* reaches its time and four roads are formed in the sky and the earth opens and the sky turns towards the west and the east is darkened; when the *katún* lays down its load on the divisions of the earth's silk cotton trees and Mayapán weeps, Standard of the Deer, Maycú, Deer Owl, and its lineage is established in well and cave, when deer die (victims) and there are fly maggots at the close of the *katunes,* at the doubling of the *katun;* when the *katunes* have delivered their burdens of sorrow and glory and confound good and evil, day and night and changes come about and the *katún* wheel of prophecy turns and all that it bears is unleashed on the earth and the Mayas suffer and are victims and through the changes that occur they become vassals, when scores of *katunes* pass without lineage and their only possesion is pain, when the passing of time brings change, after all this the Mayas will raise their heads and will speak their own words and raise their banners and will feel pride in their origins".

Muan remained seated before the vessel of pure water. He repeated the prophecies several times over. He saw how each *katún* robbed its predecessor of its Straw Mat, how new time continually filled the vacuum left by the old, how the *kines* succeeded each other. He reflected on the burden borne by the bearers of time and he looked into the future when the Mayas would be a subject people of the beared foreigners. Muan plunged a clay statutte into the jar of water, the clay became soft and he muttered to himself: "Not in vain do we hew stone, our hearts are not of clay, we leave something lasting. The temples will speak of us, stone raised up today and fallen tomorrow will speak eloquently of the magnificence of our people. For as long as Kin, the sun, continues to light the days, something of the Mayas will ever shine forth through time. Let the wheel of prophecy turn, let time turn, let the gods hide themselves and reappear when their time is come".[1]

---

[1] Fragments appearing in the last chapter were take from the Wheel of Prophecy of the Years of *Katún 5 Ahau* which was obtained through the reconstruction of the Chilam Balam of Tizimín and the Pérez Codex.

Glossary

Ahau:
Name of month. Also means Lord.

Ahau Can:
Serpent Lord and highest priest.

Ahau Chamehes:
Deity of Medicine.

Ah Buluc Ch'abtan:
The Eleven faster.

Acanum:
Protective deity of hunters.

Acehpek:
Dogs used for deer hunting.

Ah Caboob:
Inspectors responsible for administering tax matters.

Ah Can Ek:
The four darkness.

Ah Cantzicnal:
Aquatic deity, the Pourer of the Four Corners.

Ah Cap Uach Tun:
He who orders the *tunes*.

Ah Chhuy Kak:
God of violent death and sacrifice.

Ah Chichic Soot:
He who shakes the timbrel.

Ahcit Dzamalcum:
Protective god of fishermen.

Ah Cup Cacap:
God of the underworld, he who denies air, he who deprives of breath.

Ah Dzuudz:
He who is haggard.

Ah Itzam:
The water witch.

Ah Kak Nexoy:
Protective deity of fishermen.

Ah Kay Kin Bak:
He who sells meat by day.

Ah kines:
Priests, lords who consult the oracles, celebrate ceremonies and preside over sacrifices.

Ah Maax Cal:
The prattling monkey.

Ah Maycuy:
The chestnut deer.

Ah Muzencaboob:
Deities related to the *uayeb* or fateful days.

Ah Ox Kokol Tzek:
The three piler of skulls.

Ah Paxboob:
"Those who play instruments", musicians.

Ahpuá:
God of fishing.

Ah Puch:
God of Death.

Ah Sac Dziu:
The white thrush.

Ah Tooc:
The burner.

Ah Tzay Kanche:
The sure stepping stone.

Ah Xixteel Ul:
The rugged land conch.

Ah Uaxac Yol Kauil:
The eight sacred heart.

Ah Ucte Chapat:
The Seven Centipede.

Ah Uucte Cuy:
The seven owl.

Ah Uucte Cuy:
"The Seven Owl".

Akab:
Night.

Ak'Al:
Sacred marsh where water abounds.

Bacaboob (Bacabes):
The pourers, supporters of the sky and guardians of the cardinal points, who form a single god: *Ah Cantzicnal Bacab,* the pourer of the four corners.

Balam-Acab:
Character of *quiché* mythology, second man created by the gods.

Balam-Quitzé:
Character of *quiché* mythology, first man created by the gods.

Balché:
Enebriating drink, sweetened with honey and used for ceremonies and offerings.

Batabes (Bataboob):
High officials.

Batzi chuj:
Cochineal, parasite used for dying.

Bexelac:
Turtle shell used as a percussion instrument.

Bil:
Hairless dog reared for food.

Bolontikú:
Gods of death, the Nine Lords of the Night.

Buluc An:
Eleven carved stone.

Buluc Ch'abtan:
The eleven faster.

Catracán:
Character of *quiché* mythology, son of *Vucub-Caquix,* who claimed to be the shaker of the sky and the earth. Was vanquished by *Hanahpú* and *Ixbalanqué.*

Caculhá-Huracán:
The first of the gods to form the Heart of the Sky according to *quiché* mythology.

Camalotz:
Zoomorphic character of *quiché* mythology, who descended to cut off the heads of the men of wood who were imperfect beings.

Cayum:
Clay timbrel.

Cihuateteo:
Women-godesses who became divine through death

in child brith (Nahuatl word).

Cihuatlapan:
"Place of Women" (Nahuatl word).

Cit Bolon Tun:
Deity of medicine.

Cit Bolon Ua:
The Decider of Lies, god of the underworld.

Cit Chac Coh:
God of War.

Cocó kabá:
The nickname.

Cotzbalam:
Zoomorphic character of *quiché* mythology who devoured the men of wood who were imperfect beings.

Cumhú:
Name of a month.

Cutz:
Wild turkey.

Cutzha:
Duck.

Cuy:
Small black bird.

Chaac:
God of rain and of agriculture.

Chac Bolay Can:
The butcher serpent living in the underworld.

Chaces:
Priest's assistants in agricultural and other ceremonies.

Chac Hubil Ahau:
The very rebellious red lord.

Chac Imix Che:
The Red Tree of the East.

Chacmitan Choc:
Great poverty.

Chac Xib Chaac:
One of the four gods of which *Chaac* is comprised: the Red Man of the East.

Cha té:
Black vegetable dye.

Chay:
Chaya.

Chi:
Nance.

Chic caban:
Festivity held in the month of *Xul.*

Chilames:
Prophets and interpreters of the will of the gods through various adivination practices.

Chipi-Caculhá:
The second of the gods making up the Heart of the Sky in *quiché* mythology.

Chiracán Ixmucané:
The "Grandmother of Dawn", ancient augur who through the reading of grains of maize suggested that man should be made of wood, in *quiché* mythology.

Chi té:
Eugenia, plant for dying.

Ch'oh:
Indigo.

Chohom:
Dance performed in ceremonies during the month of *Zip,* related to fishing.

Choo:
Fibre extracted from the silk cotton tree.

Chul:
Flute.

Chultún:
Drinking water cistern.

Chumuc ákab:
Midnight.

Chumuc kin:
Midday.

Chunkin:
Midday.

Dzamul:
Meddler.

Dzidzontun:
Place of stones painted like hooves.

Ek:
Dye.

Ek Chuah:
Protective deity of the sowers of cocao and gods of War.

Ek Imix Che:
The Black Tree of the West.

Ek Xib Chaac:
One of the four component gods of *Chaac:* the Black Man of the West.

Emelkin:
Sunset.

Emkú:
Ceremony of puberty.

Ex:
Loin cloth.

Gucumatz:
One of the progenitor gods of *quiché* mythology. He is identified with Quetzalcóatl.

Ha:
Cocao seed.

Haab:
Solar calendar of 360 days which is made up with five extra days of misfortune which complete the final month.

Hadzab:
Wooden swords.

Halach uinic:
Leader.

Hatcab kin:
First hours of day.

Hetzmek:
Ceremony when the child is first carried astride the hip.

Hobnil Bacab:
The bee god, protector of bee keepers.

Hoh:
Crow.

Holcanes:
"The brave", warriors charged with obtaining slaves for sacrifice. (Feature of the post-classic era).

Holkan okot:
Martial dance performed especially in ceremonies during the month of *Pax*.

Holpop:
"He who sits on the rush mat", official looking after the sacred instruments.

Hom:
Trumpet.

Hunab Ku:
Giver of life, builder of the universe and father of Itzamná.

Hunahpú:
Young god of *quiché* mythology who defeated the proud *Vacub-Caquix,* who believed himself to be the sun, and his sons *Zipacná* and *Cabracán.*

Hunahpú-Utiú:
One of the "Grandfathers of Dawn" of *quiché* mythology.

Hunahpú-Vuc:
One of the "Grandfathers of the Dawn" of *quiché* mythology.

Ic:
Chili.

Ichaansihó:
Face of the birth of the sky.

Icim:
Owl.

Ik:
God of the wind.

Iqui-Balam:
Character of *quiché* mythology: fourth man created by the gods.

Itz:
Sweet potato.

Itzamná:
Lord of the Skies, creator of the beginning, god of time.

Itz-tahté:
Strongly scented resin used by women for body painting.

Ixbalanqué:
Young god of *quiché* mythology who vanquished the proud *Vacub-Caquix,* who believed himself to be the sun, and his sons *Zipacná* and *Cabracán.*

Ixchel:
Lunar godess of birth, of fertility and of medicine, inventor of spinning.

Ix Dziban Yol Nicté:
"Flower of the painted heart".

Ix Kan Itzam Tul:
The precious witch of flowing water.

Ixpiyacoc:
The "Grandmother of the Dawn" augur who rubbed the stalk of the *tzité* and suggested that man should be formed of wood, according to *quiché* mythology.

Ixtab:
Godess of the cord and of suicides by hanging.

Ix Tan Yol Ha:
The corpulent Zaraguey.

Izmucané:
One of the "Grandfathers of the Dawn" according to *quiché* mythology.

Jaleb:
Hairless dog.

Kaat Naat:
"The questioner", he who examined those being initiated in the mysteries of religion.

Kabal:
Primitive method employed by potters which consists of shaping the clay while revolving the platform on which it is placed with the foot.

Kabaxbuul:
A cooked meal containing black beans which is eaten at dusk when it was customary to eat the the heaviest meal of the day.

Kah:
Pinole flour.

Kan ak:
Plant producing a yellow dye.

Kan Imix Che:
The Yellow Tree of the South.

Kan Xib Chaac:
One of the four gods of which *Chaac* is composed: the Yellow Man of the South.

Kayab:
Percussion instrument fashioned from turtle shell.

Kaz ákab:
Dusk.

Keh:
Deer.

Keyem:
Ground maize.

Ki:
Sisal.

Kiixpaxhkum:
Chayote.

Kikché:
Tree of which the trunk serves to fashion canoes.

Kikitzin:
Yuca.

Kin:
The sun, the day, the unity of time.

Kinich:
Face of the Sun.

Kinich Ahau:
Lord of the Eye of the Sun, name given to Itzamná understood as Lord of the Day.

Kitam:
Wild boar.

Kuché:
Red cedar.

Kukulkan:
Quetzal-serpent, "plumed serpent".

Kum:
Marrow.

K'uxub:
Annatto tree.

Macal:
A type of root.

Mahucutah:
Character of *quiché* mythology, third man created by the gods.

Makob:
Vegetable colouring producing a purple or mauve dye, according to the quantity used.

Mayacimil:
"Easy death", small pox epidemic.

May Ceh:
Deer hoof.

Metnal:
The underworld, place of the dead.

Muan:
Evil bird related to death.

Munach:
Word referring to the common woman.

Muxubbak:
Tamale.

Naal kabá:
Second name given during the *emkú* ceremony.

Nacom:
Warrior chieftain. The same name is given to the one who sacrifices and who executes.

Nacxit Xuchitl:
From the Nahuatl words, *Nacxit,* "four feet" and *xóchitl,* "flower". The combination of the words means "the god replete with beauty who walks simultaneously to the four corners of the universe". This is one of the names given to Quetzalcóatl.

Nimá-Rziís:
The lord of the green gourd, according to *quiché* mythology.

Nim-Ac:
The lord of the emerald, the jeweller, according to *quiché* mythology.

Noh Ek:
The Planet Venus.

Ochin:
Sun set.

Oc na:
Festivity of the month of *Yax*. Old idols are shattered and new ones placed in the temples. Dedicated to the gods of agriculture.

Okinal:
Dusk, afternoon.

Okot uil:
Dance performed during the *Pocán* ceremony.

Olob zab kam yax:
Festival celebrated during the month of *Mol* in honour of all the gods.

On:
Advocado pear.

Op:
Plum.

Oxlanhuntikú:
God of the heavenly planes.

Paal kaabá:
Infant name, equivalent to a nick-name.

P'ac:
Tomatoes.

Pac ché:
Wooden spatula used to scrape sisal.

Pacum Chac:
Festivity dedicated to the gods of war, celebrated during the month of *Pax*.

Pakat:
God of violent death and sacrifice.

Pauahtunes:
Deities of time, each occupying a cardinal point.

P'entac:
Word used to refer to the common man.

Pic:
Underskirt.

Piim:
Fibre extracted from the silk cotton tree.

Pitz Otz:
Vegetable colouring producing a blue dye.

Ploms:
Rich people.

Pocám:
Name of a festival celebrated during the second month of the year.

Pom:
Aromatic resin, incense. Also means sound of a fall, of a large object dropping.

Pop:
First month of the year.

Potákab:
Time before dawn.

Pucc:
Means: "land of low hills"; refers to the low architecture typical of the state of Yucatan.

Put:
Papaya.

Que:
Parrot.

Raxa-Caculhá:
The third of the gods constituting *Chaac:* the White Man of the North.

Sacbé:
White road, man-made road.

Suyen:
Square blanket.

Suyuá Than:
Hierarchic, religious language.

Taman:
Cotton plant.

Tauch:
Black zapote.

Tazon té:
Moss.

Tepeu:
One of the progenitor gods, according to *quiché* mythology.

Thul:
Rabbit.

Toncoz Ché:
Wooden spatula for scraping sisal.

Tucumbalam:
Zoomorphic character of *quiché* mythology, he who shattered and ground the bones of the men fashioned of wood who were imperfect beings.

Tunkul:
Drum.

Tupp Kak:
Rite related to the Tzolkin, which was carried out during the propitiatory celebrations for agriculture during the month of *Keh*.

Tzamá:
Black bean.

Tzo:
Domestic turkeys.

Tzolkin:
Ritual calendar of 260 days.

Uah:
Tortillas, maize pancakes.

Uayeb:
Last month of the year, completed with five fateful days.

Uayeyaboob:
Patron gods of the fateful days.

Uech:
Unidentified animal.

Uh:
The moon.

Uo:
Second month of the year.

Utiú:
Coyote.

Uuc Chapac:
Seven Centipede.

Uuc Stay:
Deity of the underworld, possessor of seven forces making him the most rapid of the gods.

Xaman Ek:
Protective deity of travellers and merchants (the Polar Star).

Xanab:
Sandals.

Xcá:
Marrow.

Xcolibul:
Black bean.

Xecotcovach:
Zoomorphic character of *quiché* mythology who dug out the eyes of the men who were fashioned of wood because they were imperfect beings.

Xicul:
Sleeveless jacket decorated with feathers.

Xoox:
Shark.

Xul:
Stake with pointed, fire-hardened tip.

Ya:
Zapote.

Yá:
Zapote tree.

Yac:
Mountain cat.

Yahalcab:
The dawn.

Yaxum:
Green bird, mythological.

Yich-kaan:
Plant for dying.

Yum Kimil:
God of death.

Yuntún:
Slings.

Za:
Maize drink.

Zacatán:
Large cylindrical drum, made from a hollowed trunk with a single opening covered with hide.

Zac Imix Che:
The White Tree of the North.

Zec:
Spirit lords of beehives.

Zip:
Third month of the year.

Zipacná:
Character of *quiché* mythology, son of *Vacub-Caquix* who claimed to be creator of the mountains and the earth. Vanquished by *Hunahpú* and *Ixbalanqué*.

Zuhuyzipitzbai:
Protective deity of hunters.

Zazhal ab:
The Dawn.

Numbers:

hun: one

ca: two

ox: three

can: four

ho: five

uac: six

uuc: seven

uacax: eight

bolon: nine

lahun: ten

buluc: eleven

lahca: twelve

oxlahum: thirteen

canlahum: fourteen

holahun: fifteen

uaclahun: sixteen

uuclahun: seventeen

uacaclahun: eighteen

bolontahun: nineteen

hunkal: twenty

Periods of time:

kin: one day

uinal: 20 days

tun: 360 days

katun: 7,200 days

pictun: 2,880,000 days

calabtun: 57,600,000 days

kinchililtun:
01,152,000,000 days

alautun: 23,040,000,000 days

Days in chronological order:

Ik, Akbal, Kan, Chicchan, Kimi, Manik, Lamat, Muluc, Oc, Chuen, Eb, Ben, Ix, Men, Kib, Caban, Eznab, Cauac, Ahau, Imix.

Months in chronological order:

Pop, Uo, Zip, Zotz, Tzec, Xul, Yaxkin, Mol, Chen, Yax, Zac, Keh, Mac, Kankin, Muan, Pax, Kayab, Cumhu, Uayeb.

Other titles in the **PANORAMA** series

HISTORY

HISTORY OF MEXICO
From pre-Hispanic times to the present day
Stella M. González
Carmen G. Blázquez.

THE CONQUEST OF MEXICO
From the time of the arrival of the first
expeditiom on the Yucatan coast, to the end
of the Aztec Empire
Fernando Orozco Linares

GUERRILLEROS OF MEXICO
Famous historical figures and their exploits
from the Independence to the Mexican Revolution
Luis Garfias Magaña

Other titles in the **PANORAMA** series

THE MEXICAN REVOLUTION
A historical political-military compendium
Luis Garfias Magaña

TRUTH AND LEGEND ON PANCHO VILLA
Life and deeds of the famous leader of the
Mexican Revolution
Luis Garfias Magaña

ARCHAEOLOGY AND ANTHROPOLOGY

THE GREAT CULTURES OF MESO-AMERICA
From man's arrival on the American Continent
to the last of the Prehistoric Cultures
Demetrio Sodi M.

THE MAYAS
Life, culture and art through the experiences
of a man of the time
Demetrio Sodi M.

CODICES OF MEXICO
And their extraordinary history
María Sten

PREHISPANIC GODS OF MEXICO
Myths and deities from Nahualt Mythology.
Adela Fernández

ART

MURAL PAINTING OF MEXICO
The pre-Hispanic epoch, the Viceroyalty and the
great artists of our century
Rafael Carrillo Azpeitia

POSADA AND MEXICAN ENGRAVING
From the famous engraver of popular themes
to contemporary artists
Rafael Carrillo Azpeitia

Other titles in the **PANORAMA** series

POPULAR ART

POPULAR ART OF MEXICO
The artistic creativity of the Mexican people
throughout time
Porfirio Martínez Peñaloza

TRADITIONS

MEN AND HORSES OF MEXICO
History and practice of "Charrería"
José Alvarez del Villar

TITLES BEING PREPARED

INDIAN COSTUMES OF MEXICO
Its evolution, from prehispanic times
to the present
Ruth D. Lechuga

Printed by:
Editora de Periódicos, S.C.L.
La Prensa
División Comercial
Prolongación de Pino, 577
Col. Arenal 02980 México, D.F.
3000 copies
Mexico City, March. 1987